Why Harrison and Simmonds ?

The story of a Family Business
and what went before.

By

Anne T. Simmonds

Published
By
Harrison and Simmonds
80 High Street
Bedford
MK40 1NN

Printed and bound by RPM PRINT & DESIGN
2-3 Spur Rd, Quarry lane, Chichester, West Sussex, PO19 8PR

I dedicate this book especially to my dear husband
Michael Simmonds
And to all the Simmonds Family
who have been such an important part of my life for
over forty years, in gratitude and affection.

Anne T. Simmonds

AUTHOR'S NOTE OF THANKS

My thanks to all the people who have talked to me of their memories of Harrison and Simmonds. My especial thanks to David Simmonds for allowing me to study the old summary books and to all the different friends and relations who have helped and encouraged me during the past few years as the project has taken shape.

I interviewed Phyllis King, nee Hayward, later Bustin, in 1988 just for interest as a family historian. Phyllis has since died and her memories on the tape recorder have added greatly to the history of the early days of Harrison and Simmonds.

I am very grateful to the Surrey History Centre for their help with the records of Princess Mary's Village Homes and the staff picture. They were also a great help with the records of the London Orphan Asylum (later Reed's school.) Likewise to Marianne Thorne Archivist of the Infant Orphan Asylum (later Wanstead school) for those records. My special thanks to Peter Daniels of Active UK (Visual Communications) Ltd., for his suggestions of old Harrison Business photos etc. He supplied the J. P. Harrison baby advert and also the photos of J. P. Harrison & Son and of Edgar Harrison's shop.

My thanks to the publishers of Dan Maskell's book, and the various newspaper publishers for permission to quote from them. My thanks to Neville Cullingford of the Royal Observer Corps Museum in Southampton for the Observer Corps pictures and information.

My special gratitude for their time and memories go to Elizabeth Crathearn nee Leahy, Una Davies, Joan & Rita French, Michael & Hilary Harrison, Phyllis King, Sally Linklater, Jane Long, Michael March, John Maund, Brian Morris, Michael Mortimer, Pat Mousley, David Simmonds, Dominic Simmonds, Elizabeth Simmonds, John Simmonds (Father Simon OFM), Bro Peter Simmonds SDB, Marian Taylor and especially to my husband Michael Simmonds for his encouragement and help in so many different ways.

My apologies if I have omitted a name, but my thanks also to all in Harrison and Simmonds for their kindness and hospitality over the many years I have been made welcome there.

Anne T. Simmonds

Chapters and Illustrations

1   How I became involved

On 21st. May 2008 the family business of 'Harrison and Simmonds' begins its eightieth year of service to the people of Bedford. I first saw the shop in 1963 after I began going out with Michael Simmonds. At that time I was working as a staff nurse in the operating theatre of the Luton and Dunstable Hospital. I had met Michael, in January of 1963, through the Secular Franciscan Order, a religious organisation of which we are both members,

David, Nat & Michael Simmonds 1963

Now, after going out with him for some months, I was to stay the weekend with his family. On a Friday afternoon in September, I came by train into the old Bedford Midland Road station and following the instructions I had been given by Michael walked right along Midland Road into the town centre, turned left into the High Street and came to 'Harrison and Simmonds' a small narrow tobacconist shop half way up on the left hand side. I saw Michael behind the counter and was introduced to his brother David and their father 'Nat'. In front of the counter was old Johnny Cox, exchanging banter and laughing and wheezing as he puffed at his cigarettes.

The shop was always full of laughter. Many of the customers were known by name. The staff often had the request ready almost before the customer had asked for it. The shop consisted of a single counter on the left side with rows of tobacco jars and cigarettes etc. in fixtures behind. The jars had names like Captain Cuttle, Pickwick and Scrooge. There was a pair of scales and the staff were often weighing out amounts of different tobaccos and blending them together to fill the various jars.

I later learnt that these were Nat's own blends that he had created and called after Dickens characters, as he was very fond of Dickens books. There were showcases on the right that displayed lighters and cigarette boxes etc. There was nothing in the shop in those days that was not connected with tobacco, except the Crucifix over the door that proclaimed the Christianity of the family.

When it was time for the shop to close I went out to 'The Moorings', 112 Bromham Road, Biddenham with Michael in his little Austin A30 and David took Nat home in his little Morris. I was welcomed and shown around by Madeleine, Michael's mother and we all ate together. I was surprised when his wife referred to Nat as 'Harrison' and I was told this was his second name. He was generally Nat in the shop and Harrison in the family.

There was a lot of joking and puns being capped by worse puns. I often wish I could remember them all. The cheese was in a large dish on the sideboard. Harrison had a habit of saying; 'Would anyone like some cheese?' and when someone moved to get some he would say 'Get me some while you are there please!' I gathered that Harrison was very proud of the fact that he had been born in Mitre House in Salisbury. At that time I had no idea what that meant.

After the meal Michael took me out to do a collection round that he did for the Church. On our return I was bedded down on the studio couch in the sitting room. We all retired to sleep but in the middle of the night there was a violent thunderstorm. I was standing at the window looking out at the storm when there was a knock at the door. Madeleine had come down to make sure I was not frightened by the storm. We had a nice chat over a cup of tea and when the storm died down we retired back to bed.

In the morning Michael and David knew nothing of the storm, they had slept right through it! Michael & I set off, soon after seven am, to go to Holy Child & St.Joseph church for Mass at 7-30am and then to the shop. He bought two Cornish pasties, hot from the oven, from Canvin's and we ate them for our breakfast, with a welcome cup of tea, in the tiny office cum kitchen at the back of the shop, before the shop opened at 8-30am.

I was introduced to Peggy Canny in the shop; she was Harrison's Goddaughter and a great friend as well as a valued employee. Later Harrison arrived having been driven into Bedford by Madeleine and she took me back out to Biddenham. We spent the day picking apples off the trees in the orchard and talking. They had a smallholding beside the river Great Ouse near the old bridge that leads into Bromham. There were two long Nissan huts behind the house. One was used as a garage and workshop and in the other Madeleine kept over 100 chickens in deep litter. The eggs were wonderful, full of flavour with deep yellow yolks. When lunchtime approached I helped Madeleine cook two relays of dinners, as the shop did not close at lunchtime. David brought his Dad home for the early lunch soon after 12 and Michael came an hour later.

This was the pattern, the shop and Church and home life all mixed together in every day. On Sunday we went to Mass and Michael's Aunt Ede and her daughter Pat came to lunch. There was a lot of good-natured banter and teasing and it was obviously a very close family. Later in the day Michael drove me back to Luton after a very happy weekend.

My relations were becoming curious to know Michael. My parents and siblings were living in Arild in the south of Sweden at that time as my father was working over there, so the family in England were my Grandmother and Aunt Marian who lived in Luton. They were my father's mother and sister. We arranged for Michael to come over and have tea with the Taylor's. He arrived laden with gifts: a box of apples, a jar of his mother's home made jam and a large bunch of flowers from her garden, made a good impression before he even said 'Hello'. He was introduced and left to talk to Grandma while Aunt Marian & I got the tea laid. During tea Marian said we would probably have to sit in the dark later as the fuse had gone.

Michael immediately offered to mend it, so he crawled into the cupboard under the stairs with a candle and mended the fuse. When he emerged he had red candle wax on his sleeve. Marian was very concerned but Michael said 'Oh don't worry it will soon come out with blotting paper and a hot iron.'

Later he was introduced to the vagaries of a faulty cistern in the cloakroom so he climbed up on to the toilet seat and adjusted the stopcock. Marian was so grateful, she said to me over the washing up, 'Anne, he's a gem! Hang on to him! If I was forty years younger I would have him myself!'

The next day Marian went to Broadmead school, where she was a nursery teacher and the school secretary, Mrs Berrett who had known me since I was tiny, asked how they had got on with the new boyfriend. Marian's reply: 'Oh we had a wonderful time; we spent half the time in the cupboard under the stairs and the rest of the time standing on the lavatory seat!'

In early November, Michael asked me to marry him and he bought me a beautiful opal ring. I bought him a signet ring and we had them blessed at the meeting of the Secular Franciscan Order, by Father Callistus OFM on 11th November 1963. Michael took me to see the 'Sound of Music' at the Dominion Theatre in London to celebrate and I spent many more happy weekends with the Simmonds family.

A few weeks before this, I had come out of the library in Luton and was surprised to see my father Hugh Taylor standing at a bus stop opposite. I did not know he was in England, never mind Luton! So I went over and said 'Hullo Dad; what are you doing here?' He told me that he had been for an interview in Birmingham and that if he got the job the family were going to come back to live in England again after eight years in Sweden. I was thrilled and so were Grandma and Auntie Marian.

I left the Luton & Dunstable Hospital just after Christmas and moved into Bedford Hospital to work in the operating theatre of Bedford South Wing. Michael came over to Luton on New Years Eve and brought me, with all my belongings, to the new Nurse's home at Bedford Hospital South Wing. During the journey he told me that his father was not at all well.

On my first day 1 January 1964, I was told to go to Matron's office at eight am, before starting work. Matron came striding down the corridor and greeted me with 'Well Nurse Taylor! What an introduction to the hospital! To have your future father-in-law on the table before you've even started!' My brain just said, 'How on earth did she know he was my future father-in-law!'

Harrison had been admitted during the night with a perforated ulcer in his stomach and had an emergency operation. I was in the operating theatre a few days later when he had a second operation. He was off work for about six weeks but soon recovered and was back at the shop as usual before Easter.

My father Hugh G. Taylor came to work in Birmingham in January 1964 and he came and visited Michael's family. Hugh got on very well with

Harrison and Madeleine and we all had a happy day together both in the shop and in Biddenham.

David, Michael, Hugh Taylor & Nathaniel Simmonds

Hugh was searching for a house in Birmingham for the family who were staying in Sweden until the summer so my brother Kevin could take his 'Real Examen.' (The equivalent of our GCSE exams.)

Michael and I also started house hunting and after looking at various houses we eventually decided on a 3 bed-roomed semi-detached house in Chestnut Avenue, Queen's Park, which was within walking distance of the Church, and the new Catholic school, St Josephs, that was being built in Chester Road. We were all pleasantly surprised at Easter when David Simmonds announced his engagement to Liliane Pace.

My brother John was at sea working as a steward on a cargo boat. His ship was coming into Liverpool in the spring, so it was arranged that he would come down and visit us. Michael and I met the train in Bedford Midland Station and were disappointed when no John alighted. We went back to Biddenham without him and wondered what had happened.

Peggy was working in the shop and had heard that my brother had not arrived. She saw a young man walk past looking in, then she saw him again looking over from the far side of the High Street.

John Taylor, Madeleine & Michael Simmonds with Mary Shiner and her boys. Spring 1964

When he went past the third time she ran out, tapped him on the shoulder and asked, 'Are you Anne Taylor's brother?' He said in amazement 'Yes I am; how did you know?'

We got a phone call from Peggy at the shop and joyfully drove in to Bedford to fetch John. He had gone to sleep on the train and had woken up at St Pancras station! John knew that Michael's name was Simmonds but not the name of the shop! We were told then that it was Harrison and Simmonds because Harrison's Uncle, Ernie Harrison, had been the senior partner in the shop when it first started.

We had a happy day out at "The Moorings" with Michael's sister Mary and her five little boys, Nicholas, Francis, Richard, Bernard and Stephen as well as Madeleine and Michael. Mary was married to a farmer Ernest Shiner and they lived out at Cranfield. We learned that Michael & Mary had two older brothers Peter and John. Peter was a missionary in Cape Town, South Africa, and John was a Franciscan Lay Brother working in Yorkshire.

Our wedding was planned for August 3rd 1964, a Bank Holiday Monday, because the shop would be closed. David & Liliane planned their wedding for 10th September, a Thursday afternoon, early closing day, thus allowing the family members who worked in the shop to attend the wedding.

Michael & I had a very happy day with my Dad, now living in Birmingham, at my cousin Joan Taylor's wedding in Luton, to her fiancé Robin Whittle in May. The spring ran into summer and I went back and forth to Luton for fittings of my Wedding dress that Auntie Marian was making for me. I finished work at the hospital a week or so before our wedding.

Hugh & Anne Taylor with Michael Simmonds at Joan Taylor's wedding reception. 9th May 1964

We welcomed my mother Aideen and brothers, John 18, and Kevin 16 and my little sister Clare, just 11, who all arrived from Sweden four days before the wedding. My sister Mary 22 was already married in Sweden with two small children so could not come.

The family all moved with me into the little house at 26 Chestnut Avenue where Michael & I were to live. My Parents slept in the double bed that would be ours later. It had been a gift from Michael's Aunt Nell and we had bought a new mattress to go on it. Clare had the spare bed in the little room. The boys slept in sleeping bags in the empty back bedroom and I slept downstairs on the studio couch, which had been given to us by Michael's parents. Michael was still sharing a room at the Moorings with his brother David.

The night before the wedding my Mum insisted that I should sleep in the spare room and Clare sleep on the couch. Mummy said 'We cannot have the bride on a couch in the living room!'

John brought me breakfast in bed on my wedding morning. He had cooked me scrambled eggs and crisp bacon, with toast and tea. Lovely!

I went down in my dressing gown to greet my Granddad Hood and his wife Lizzie (Mum's dad and stepmother) before donning my wedding dress and veil. Aunt Marian had made my dress from white satin brocade woven with a pattern of lilies of the valley. I had a circular veil and a little wreath of lilies of the valley with pearl leaves. My sister Clare was my bridesmaid, wearing a pale yellow dress that my Mum had made for her.

Dear old Daisy Doubleday was playing the organ and I was in the porch of Holy Child & St.Joseph Church, with my Dad having endless photograph's taken by my Uncle Ted, when the wedding march began and I said, 'Come on Dad, its time.' As I walked down the aisle with my Father, I was surprised at the numbers of people that were in the church. Our wedding day was very hot and the service went well.

Canon Anthony Hulme, Michael & Anne, Bro Simon OFM (John) Simmonds, Clare Taylor & Father Anthony Sketch. August 3rd. 1964.

The Parish priest Canon Anthony Hulme gave a commentary on the service for the benefit of our non-Catholic relations, as most of the service was in Latin.

Father Anthony Sketch, the curate, who had been at school with Michael said the Wedding Mass. Brother Simon (Michael's brother John) assisted Father Sketch. David was Michael's best man.

Our wedding reception was held at 87 Goldington Road at the home of Michael's Aunt Ede, where she had big rooms and a big garden. A friend of Michael's had made the Wedding cake and all went off very well.

Most of the guests were in the garden and at one point Michael and I just collapsed onto the couch in the front room, just glad to sit down for five minutes. My Uncle Ted (my dad's elder brother) was the photographer and Michael's best friend Michael Mortimer drove us to the station to go away on our honeymoon.

My family stayed in our future home until two days after the wedding. With Madeleine's help they cut up the wedding cake and sent it out in little boxes, to all the relations who could not be there. They then travelled up to Yardley, Birmingham, to start their new life there.

Michael and I had a ten days honeymoon touring the Shrines of France. When we returned to 26 Chestnut Avenue, Madeleine had made up our bed and prepared a meal for us and left it cooking slowly in the oven. She had even set the table for us. There was a large pile of wedding presents beautifully arranged waiting for us to open. It was a happy homecoming.

I had decided to finish work because the hospital's idea of part time was nine to five on five days a week, and Michael was used to coming home for his midday meal. I did not think he should have to change his life because I wanted to work.

We all enjoyed David & Liliane's wedding on 10th September and were settling down to married life when I nearly had a miscarriage. This was towards the end of October and I retired to bed leaving the washing half done. I was lying in bed after the Doctor had been and I heard Michael cycling up the road with a metal bedpan clonking in his bicycle basket! He had borrowed it from the St. John Ambulance people. He had sold his car as he said he could afford a house and a wife but not a car as well and something had to go. I spent three weeks in bed and the miscarriage was averted and our first child Bernadette Mary was born on 18th May 1965.

Madeleine and Harrison were thrilled with their first granddaughter. Soon after the weddings, Harrison & Madeleine had sold the smallholding and moved out to Bromham to live in Primrose Cottage, in Grange Lane. Madeleine loved her garden and could grow anything. Her roses were a real glory over the gate each summer. Soon after they moved, we had a visit from Michael's eldest brother Peter who was a Salesian Lay Brother working in Cape Town as a missionary.

Our first child, Bernadette was followed by Clare in September 1965 and Francis in February 1969. We had planned to call our first son Francis John and when he came we realised that he was the first Simmonds grandson as Mary's boys were all Shiners. So Francis was baptised Francis John Nathaniel, as Nathaniel is the old family name.

In 1969, Harrison and Madeleine decided to go on a cruise out to Cape Town to visit Peter. Madeleine's friend, Alice Cullen went with them and they all had a wonderful six-week holiday and really enjoyed their break.

Nathaniel Harrison and Madeleine Simmonds 1969

By this time Michael was feeling he wanted to be something more then a salesman so he applied to do teacher training. Harrison & David were sorry to see him leave the shop but encouraged him in his new vocation. Liliane's brother-in-law John Maund began to work in the shop about this time.

Early in 1970 Harrison became seriously ill with Lymphosarcoma and we all knew it was just a matter of time. In July Madeleine told me quite casually that she had to go to the hospital for some tests. She had the tests and was told to go in for an exploratory operation. After the operation we were told she might live six months, but she died ten days later on August 23rd. 1970.

We were up in Birmingham staying with my family and it was a complete shock to get a phone call saying she had died. We had visited her in the hospital the day before we left and she gave me a 10 shilling note and said 'Here is something to buy treats for the children and don't let my being ill spoil your holiday. ' I have always said that if I could have picked out my own Mother-in-law I could not have picked a better one then Madeleine. She was so kind and taught me so much.

I stayed in Birmingham for a few more days with the children and Michael went off home to see his father. He was wondering what he could say to comfort his Dad. When he arrived at Primrose Cottage, Brother Simon (John) opened the door and told Michael with a smile that he was not praying for their Mum but to her. So there was no awkwardness at all. The funeral was a beautiful thanksgiving for a wonderful life and Madeleine was laid to rest at Elstow Abbey where Michael's grandmother was buried and also the ashes of Uncle Ernie and his wife Aunt Embo.

Within three weeks of Madeleine's funeral Harrison had sold his bungalow at Bromham and moved into 87 Goldington Road with his two sisters, Edith and Nell. He had never looked after himself and he was not a well man anyway. He gave me Madeleine's solitaire ring. When we sorted her clothes etc., we found painkiller pills in every drawer and pocket. Madeleine had been suffering for a long time and never spoke of it to anyone. She was a wonderful lady.

Harrison had deferred his pension until he was 70. His 70th birthday was 9th December. He drew his pension for the first and only time on his way to the hospital and he died there a few days later on 16th December 1970. By chance Peter was at home on leave from Cape Town and he was with his father at the end. Michael had gone to fetch John, but they did not get back in time.

Harrison was joking and saying he hoped it would be a fine day for the funeral. At one point he suddenly said, 'I've seen her!' We all hoped it was Madeleine that he had seen. Harrison was buried in Elstow Abbey churchyard with Madeleine. The Shop was closed on the day of the funeral for the first time since Uncle Ernie had died in 1938.

David was now the senior partner with his brother in law, John Maund and Liliane's cousin Michael March as partners. David and Liliane have three children James, Matthew and Christiane. In 1971 we had twins Dominic and Maria. Michael was now a teacher and time passed very fast with five small children to care for.

In November 1975 we had a health crisis in which three of the children and myself were in hospital having blood transfusions within three weeks. It was because I had inherited a rare blood condition. The doctors were saying, 'Does it come from your father or your mother? How far back does it go?'

So I began to research the family history. I wanted to find out as much as I could about my children's ancestry not just my own. In my researches into my husband's ancestry the story of the business has unfolded with the story of the family.

According to family tradition the Harrison family are descended from Sir Richard Harrison of Hurst, near Reading, in Berkshire. Sir Richard raised two troops of horse for King Charles I in the Civil War and was made Lord of the Manor of Whistley and Hinton. This descent has yet to be definitely proved.

However what is definite is that there were two brothers who were in business in Buckingham in the early 1820s. James Harrison, the elder brother, was landlord of the White Hart Inn in the Market Square and he was postmaster and auctioneer. He was married to Cecilia nee Hollier and they had a family of two sons Thomas and James and three daughters, Cecilia Fanny, Sophia Martha, and Lucinda Esther

At one point the Post Office complained that James was not fulfilling all the duties of postmaster but they admitted that he had asked to be relieved of the duty. Not long after a new Post Mistress was appointed. Her name - Miss Sophia Hollier, she was James's Sister-in-law! So although he did not keep the post he kept it in the family. Later he became Bailiff of Buckingham in 1829 (similar to a Mayor.) His son James also became Bailiff and that family was prominent in the town all through the 1800's

There is a large coffin tomb in the Old churchyard cemetery that has inscriptions on four sides as follows: - 'SACRED TO THE MEMORY OF JAMES HARRISON WHO DIED 10 JUNE 1869, AGED 83 YEARS. SACRED TO THE MEMORY OF CECILIA THE WIFE OF JAMES HARRISON, WHO DIED 11TH. SEPT. 1853 AGED 70 YEARS. ALSO TO THE MEMORY OF ANNE WIFE OF JAMES HARRISON JUN. DAUGHTER OF THOMAS AND ANNE RIDGEWAY, WHO DIED 26TH MARCH 1861 AGED 56 YEARS. SACRED TO THE MEMORY OF JAMES HARRISON, JUN. WHO DIED 12TH. MAY 1882 AGED 68 YEARS.' It also gives dates of all the children's deaths etc. some who died in Birmingham.

James senior had a younger brother Richard Harrison who was a stonemason. Richard married twice, first to Mary ? about 1819 by whom he had two daughters, Eliza born August 1820 and Mary Ann who was baptised 3 September 1822 the day after her mother had died. Richard may have carved Mary's tombstone himself, it is still there in the old churchyard cemetery and easily read. It reads "IN MEMORY OF MARY HARRISON, WIFE OF RICHARD HARRISON. SHE DEPARTED THIS LIFE SEPTEMBER 2ND 1822 AGED 21 YEARS. ALSO MARY ANN DAUGHTER OF ABOVE DIED IN HER INFANCY." I expect her mother's people looked after Eliza, but we hear no more of her for many years.

In an old 'Poll book of the Election on 10th December 1832, both brothers are listed. James is a Burgess and Freeman & tenant of the Duke of Buckingham. Richard has a note saying 'Promised one way and voted another'! These were the days before the secret ballot. There is also a William Harrison listed but I don't know if he was a relation.

After five years Richard married again a lady called Pleasant Painter who had been born in Tingewick, a village just outside Buckingham. Her father John Painter's family came from Mixbury that is just over the border into Oxfordshire although it is next to Tingewick. The wedding took place on 8th November 1827 at Wootton in Oxfordshire, not far from Blenheim Palace. Pleasant was called after her grandmother who had been Pleasant Roberts. The Roberts family came from the Wootton area so that may have been why the wedding took place so far away from Buckingham. Richard and Pleasant had a large family of five boys, and two girls.

In 1851 the two families are shown in the census of Buckingham. James Harrison is down as Auctioneer and Alderman aged 65, his wife Cecilia is 67 and their daughter Cecilia is 35. They have two visitors from Cornwall and two servants. Their eldest son, also James Harrison, is Auctioneer & Estate agent aged 37, his wife is Anne and they have four children James Thomas, William, Anne and Richard. They had two servants, one a housemaid and the other a nursery maid. They later had three more children, another Cecilia, George Hollier and Lucy.

At 12 Market Square are Richard Harrison aged 55, a stone-mason employing 10 men, Pleasant his wife age 46, son Henry aged 22 also a stonemason, Joseph P. chemist and druggist aged 20, Elizabeth 18, Richard 14, Catherine 11 and John 8. They also had a son George who came between Elizabeth and Richard but he was not at home on census night.

Henry became a stonemason and later took over his father's business. Joseph Painter who was baptised on 17 August 1830, trained as a chemist and druggist. George became a grocer and in the census in 1861 he has his mother and his sister Catherine, an invalid, living with him. Pleasant is still down as married but there is no sign of Richard the father. He may have been in Hospital or he may have been staying with relations, possibly in Selly Park Birmingham. Elizabeth must have married. The youngest brother Richard was an errand boy in 1851 but by 1881 he is a reporter & accountant. I have not yet discovered what happened to Richard Harrison; I have not found his death certificate.

However on the 1881 census Pleasant Harrison aged 76 is living in Long Buckby in Northamptonshire. She is living with Eliza Tebbitt, aged 60, her stepdaughter and they are both widows. In 1871 they are not there but in both 1871 and 1881 there are lots of other Tebbitt families and also lots of Painter families in Long Buckby so we can presume that the two ladies had relations there and that is how they came to live there.

Joseph Painter Harrison

Joseph Painter Harrison moved to Salisbury, Wilts. in the late 1850's while still training as a chemist and druggist. In the evenings Joseph must have visited the George and Dragon Inn in Castle Street near to his lodgings where George Creed the Publican had six pretty daughters in his family of eight children. Joseph soon began walking out with the eldest girl.

Her name was Emily and she been called after her mother Emily Creed nee Chinn. The Creed family go back in Salisbury to the early parish registers, sometimes the name is spelt Crede, but it is all the same family. In Pepys' diaries he talks a lot about Mr. Creed and on one of his holidays, visiting Salisbury he says '*I walked by the river with Mr. Creed*' so it maybe that one of my children's ancestors was a friend of Samuel Pepys.

In the census of April 1861, Joseph P. Harrison was living alone at 29 Brew Street, Salisbury; he is 30 and a chemist's assistant.

Joseph had asked Emily to marry him and the wedding took place a few weeks after the census on Sunday June 9th 1861 at St.Thomas's Church in Salisbury.

St. Thomas's Church Salisbury where Joseph & Emily were married.

Joseph's Bible was found walled up in the Wheatsheaf Inn in Salisbury in October 1961. We have several newspaper cuttings that were published at the time. The first shows a picture of the then Landlord of the Wheatsheaf Inn, Arthur Buckden, looking at the bible, it reads:-

"The Names in the Family Bible.
There are still many Harrisons living in Salisbury and Mr. Arthur Buckton Licensee of the Wheatsheaf inn is wondering if they are descendants of a fine old Victorian family once connected with the premises. This week, workmen modernising the building, believed to be 650 years old, have discovered an old bible brown with age, in which the saga of the Sarum Harrisons is inscribed in faded ink.

Paterfamilias was J W Harrison who married Miss E. Creed at St Thomas' church on June 9, 1861. Their first child was Catherine born in March 1862, and christened at Sarum St. Edmund then came Frances born 1863 then Frederick in August 1864, followed by Annie October 1865, George Henry October 1866, and Frank Inigo September 1867. After this there were three sets of twins Edith & Ellen in November 1868, William & Arthur in 1870 and Alice and Ernest in 1871. Then came Richard in 1873 and Edgar in 1875. The Bible was found behind a mud wall which crumbled at the touch. Part of the building is believed to have been a blacksmiths shop until fairly recent times."

16

(Sarum is an old abbreviation for Salisbury.)

On December 8th there was a letter headed 'Harrison Bible.'

"Sir. Concerning the old Harrison family Bible recently found behind a mud wall in the Wheatsheaf Inn, as I am the last descendant left in Salisbury, I was extremely interested to see the old book.

My mother was Alice (Mrs Albert Burden) one of the third set of twins! She lived her whole life in the city and died four years ago at the age of 86 and a half years. I found the inscriptions- my grandfather's clear handwriting- most exacting. He died long before I was born. Not only has he recorded the dates of his 14 children's births, but also the days of the week and the times of the day they were born. Also he has entered the names of the parsons who christened them all and he recorded the sponsors of the children who were various great aunts and uncles of mine, whom I just remember. They were all wellknown citizens in their time. Mrs Polly Snook of Stratford-sub-Castle; Mr Jo Snook the butcher and Mrs Carrie Hobden, late of Roslin Belle Vue Road - all relations of my Grandmother. She was formerly Emily Creed after whom I am named.

The landlord Mr. Buckton very kindly gave me the Bible because of its sentimental value. I am most grateful to him. I shall convey the Bible safely to my only living aunt Mrs Simmonds. She is one of the first set of twins, now living in Bedford and she had her 93rd birthday last week.

Phyllis Emily Burden 22 Mill Road, Salisbury."

Later there was another letter:-

"Sir. It was most interesting to me to read the two cuttings from the Journal referring to the Harrison Family Bible as my mother Mrs Edith Simmonds who was 93 on the 22nd of last month, is the last surviving member of the Harrison Family of that generation and is the Edith of the first set of twins mentioned in your paper. Her father Mr. Joseph Painter Harrison (not J W as mentioned in your article) was, I understand the first qualified chemist in Salisbury, and was later joined by his eldest son Frederick, also a qualified chemist.

My mother married Nathaniel Simmonds, who was a bookseller at Mitre house, High Street, Salisbury where her five children were born. She has been a widow for fifty five years and when her husband died the business was taken over by his brother Henry the father of the present proprietor Harry Simmonds whose shop is now a few doors away from Mitre House.

My mother is now living with her widowed daughter at 87 Goldington Road, Bedford. Apart from being very deaf she is in good health and loves to hear any news of Salisbury.

Although I had to leave Salisbury at the tender age of five, owing to my father's death, I always tell my friends with great pride that I was born under the shadow of Salisbury Cathedral.

Nathaniel Harrison Simmonds.

The Moorings, Bromham Road, Biddenham, Beds."

How did the bible get into the wall of the Wheatsheaf Inn?

On the 1891 census I found that the family next door were William Snook, a butcher and his family. William's wife Polly nee Creed was one of Emily's sisters so there was a family connection next door. All those old houses in that part of Salisbury were built of lath and plaster, so its seems likely that the bible was put into a wall cupboard and forgotten, then found seventy years later during renovations.

Joseph entered his Wedding into his Bible as he did with all the births of his 14 children including three sets of twins. His old fashioned handwriting led to the confusion about his initial as his elaborate P does look rather like a W to modern eyes.

The full text reads as follows:-

J. P. Harrison & E. Creed married Sunday June 9th 1861
>   *St. Thos. Church Salisbury by Rev. W. Renard.*
Catherine Emily Harrison Born March 23rd 1862 9.42 am.
>   *Christened May 11th 1862 at St. Edmunds Sarum. Revd A Earle*
>   *Sponsors J P H & E H & Harriett*
Frances Elizabeth Harrison Born August 9th 1863 4.50 pm
>   *Christened Octr. 25th 1863 at St. Edmunds Sarum, Revd M. Austin.*
>   *Sponsors J P H, E H & Carrie. (Died Thursday August 18th 1864, Buried*
>   *August 22nd/ 64 in Salisbury Cemetery Grave no 360b)*
Frederick Joseph Harrison Born Monday August 1st 1864 2.18 am.
>   *Christened Sept. 4th 1864 at St. Edmunds Sarum, Revd N G Swayne*
>   *Sponsors J P H, J T Small & E H*
Annie Eliza Harrison Born Tuesday October 18th. 1865 at 6 am.
>   *Christened Nov. 5th. 1865 at St Edmunds Sarum, Revd M Shuttleworth*
>   *Sponsors J P H, E H, & Polly*
George Henry Harrison Born Wednesday Oct. 3rd 1866 3.50 am
>   *Christened Oct. 28th 1866 at St. Edmunds Sarum Revd M Shuttleworth*
>   *Sponsors J P H, J N Hobden & E H*
Frank Inigo Harrison Born Saturday Sept. 7th 1867 8 am
>   *Christened Sept. 29th 1867 at St. Edmunds Sarum Revd N G Swayne*
>   *Sponsors J P H, J N Hobden, & E H*

>   *(Edith Fanny Harrison Born Sunday Novr 22nd 1868 9.10 am*
>   *(Christened Dec. 20th. 1868 at St Edmunds Sarum Revd Shuttleworth*
Twins *(Sponsors J PH & E H & Mrs Collins*
>   *(Ellen Harrison born Novr 22nd. 1896 10.15 am.*
>   *(Christened Dec. 20th. 1868 at St Edmunds Sarum. Revd Shuttleworth*
>   *(Sponsors J P H, E H, & Mrs Butler*

Twins
(William John Harrison Born Monday May 2nd /70 3.55 am
(Christened May 29th / 70 St. Edmunds Sarum Revd Jackman.
(Sponsors J P H & E H & M Collins.
(Died Sunday Aug. 8/70
(Buried Sept 2/70 at Salisbury Cemetery (Grave 361b)
(Arthur Richard Harrison Born Monday May 2nd 4.5 am
(Christened May 29th. /70 at St. Edmunds Sarum Revd Jackman
(Sponsors J P H & E H & M Collins.
(Died Thurs Sept 1st/70
(Buried Sept 2nd /70 at Salisbury Cemetery (Grave 361b)
(Born in house in London Road in parish of Whitford.

Twins
(Alice Harrison Born Saturday June 24th /71 7am
(Christened July 23rd. 71 St. Edmonds (Sarum Revd. Huish
(Sponsors J P H, W. Snook, E H & Polly.
(Ernest Harrison Born Saturday June 24th./71 7.10 am
(Christened July 23rd. /71 St. Edmunds Sarum, Revd. Huish
(Sponsors J P H, W. Snook, E H & Polly
(Born at no 18 Elm Grove Terrace, Parish of St Martins.

Richard Sydney Harrison Born Thursday Novr 20th /73 7.3 am.
Christened Sunday December 14th /73 at St. Paul's Fisherton Revd E A
Thwaits Rector. Sponsors J P H. E H. & G Purton.
(Born 29 Fisherton St,)
Edgar John Harrison Born Tuesday Febry 9th /75 10.15 pm.
Christened Sunday March 14th./75 At St.Paul's Fisherton. Rev. Jno.
McKay Curate. Sponsors J P H, E H & W Snook.
(Born at 29 Fisherton Street)

What a family! Imagine losing your toddler when you have a two-week-old new baby! And coping with twin babies when you already have five children! I only had three children when I had our twins and it was hard work although also a lot of fun. It is amazing that Emily survived all those births and lived to a ripe old age. She must have been tough.

In April 1871 the family are living at 18 London Road, Milford, in the parish of St. Edmund's Salisbury. The children are Catherine 9, Frederick 6, Annie 5, George 4, Frank 3 and Edith and Ellen 2. There is also

19

a servant girl of 16 called Emily Alexander. Joseph is still a Chemists Assistant.

Imagine all the washing for that large family all done by hand with no washing machines or dryers! By 1881 they were living at 29 Fisherton St. Salisbury where Joseph now had his own Chemist shop. The family is now complete with three more children listed Alice 10, Richard 7 and Edgar 6. The older ones are all ten years older. Ernest 10, Alice's twin, was living in The Close of the Cathedral, as he was a Chorister of the Cathedral.

Back: Edith Fanny, Frank Inigo, Frederick Joseph, George Henry, Ellen,
Front: Ernest, Alice, Catherine Emily, Joseph Painter, Edgar John, Emily,
Annie Eliza, & Richard Sydney Harrison. Circa 1886.

Joseph Painter Harrison was one of the first chemists to be registered with the Royal Pharmaceutical Society on 1st October 1868; his address was just given as Salisbury. Family tradition says he was the first fully qualified chemist in Salisbury.

In 1872 Joseph's address was given as 29 Fisherton Street, Salisbury and he remained there until his death in 1894. The window of the shop would have been full of large glass containers in various colours that would have instantly identified the shop as a chemist. In those days Chemist shops sold a lot of patent medicines, invalid and infant foods. The prescriptions were mainly in powder form that would have to be carefully measured out

and individually wrapped. The pills would have been rolled by h_____.
Many of the drugs would have been prescribed in medicines that were
dispensed in coloured bottles, with hand written labels. Poisons were kept
in green bottles that were ridged vertically so that they would be
distinguished by touch as well as by sight, to prevent mistakes.

BABIES THRIVE ➤
ON
HARRISON'S FOOD.

IT IS THE BEST AND CHEAPEST.

FOR

FREE Sample Tin and full particulars send
a post card to Proprietors.

J. P. HARRISON & SON,
Manufacturing Chemists (Examination)

29, Fisherton Street, SALISBURY.

One of the advertisements for baby food, from that time supplied by Peter
Daniels of Salisbury

The shop would also have sold candles, sauces, pickles, tea, cocoa,
matches, tobacco and even seeds and aerated water. Inside would have
been rows of small drawers and lots of bottles with labels, also different
sizes of scales, lots of assorted measuring glasses and different sizes of
pestles and mortars. Some chemists mixed their own perfumes and they
sold toiletries such as hair dressings, lotions, perfumed soaps, cold cream
and tooth powders and pastes. They also sold measuring glasses and
spoons of different sizes and types, and babies' bottles. Another line would
have been bedpans, urinals, feeding cups and thermometers and other
nursing equipment, because in those days most sick people were nursed at
home by their own relations.

Joseph Painter Harrison died on 15th October 1893, aged 63 years,
the death certificate states that he had 'albumenuria 16 years' and 'optic
neuritis' 3 months. This means he had some kidney troubles, and towards

the end eye problems. His death was registered by his eldest son, Frederick Joseph, who was 'present at the death at 29 Fisherton Street, Salisbury.'

This poem was published as the last poem in a book called "Chords Major and Minor" by another son Frank Inigo Harrison. It seems right to include it here.

In Memoriam.
J. P. H. October 15th 1894

The golden rays of morning sun , Shone bright o'er him whose work was done;
The fight was fought, the race was run, The rest he sought was well nigh won

And now he saw the closing way; Before him rose eternal day,
Death's "Vale of Shadow" dark'ning lay: Shall fear prevail? Say, Father, "Nay."

He passed in faith beyond death's dream, And gazed in awe on heaven's gleam,
Beheld his Saviour "Welcome" beam, Who bade him fear not cross the stream

And standing thus to Christ so nigh, He called each one and said "Good-bye"
His face the while transformed with joy, Committing all to God on high.

And strength beyond this world's was given, To him who firm in faith had striven;
And, ere the chord of life was riven, He blessed us all in sight of heaven

Brief Vision blest, the veil is rent; Moments on shore eternal spent!
Oh God, to us may grace be sent To tread the path by which he went.

Each day of life, may that last prayer, Recall a loving father's care;
And, God do Thou our hearts prepare To share with him Thy Presence there.

Frank Inigo Harrison

Joseph left a Will that was signed on 31st January 1894. He left the Chemist business to Frederick Joseph with a share for his wife Emily. He left all wines, liquors etc for Emily's personal use and the house and its contents in trust for Emily's use as long as she lived and to be divided between all his children after her death.

He named Frederick Joseph as his chief executor. He left £25 to Catherine, and £40 to Annie 'as she had not been put to a business,' the residue was to be divided between all his children. His 'Effects totalled £807.11s.7d'. which was quite a good sum in those days.

Maybe among the customers of the chemist shop would have been old William Simmonds and his son Nathaniel Simmonds. William had been born in 1798, he was baptised with his sister Sarah on 19 December 1799 at St. Martin's Church, Salisbury, so he may have been a twin. Little Sarah died and was buried on 18 August 1800 at the same church. William and Sarah, his parents, had three more children; Thomas, another Sarah, and Mary Ann, who were all baptised in Fisherton Anger on 25 December 1810.

William became a fellmonger and his son Nathaniel a currier. A fellmonger is similar to a tanner working with skins but the tanner only works with cow skins to make leather. The fellmonger works with sheepskins and other hides. He would go up on the fells to skin the sheep and thus got his name. The currier has gone a stage further; he uses lots of special knives to make the prepared skins thin and soft and supple to make kid gloves etc.

William had married in 1824 a lady called Isabella Norris who came from the village of Newton Tony in Wiltshire. In the census of 1841 they are living at Dyers Court, Fisherton Anger, on the edge of Salisbury. They are shown with Thomas 14, Mary 11, Henry 9, Nathaniel 7, Pamela 5 and Richard 1 year old, all born in Wiltshire. Further along in Fisherton Street are listed another William Simmonds aged 65 with Sarah aged 60; these are quite likely to be our William's parents.

The 1851 census shows more details of the family. They are at 16 Fisherton Street, Fisherton Anger. William is 53, a Fellmonger, Isabella is 49, Thomas, 25, is also a fellmonger, Henry, 20, is a shoemaker, Pamela, 15, is a Mantua maker, Matilda, 9 and Richard, 11, are scholars. The children were all born in Fisherton Anger. Nathaniel, 16, is a currier servant living in Milford with a Thomas Brown, 60, a currier, and a domestic servant called Hannah Whitlock aged 25.

Nathaniel's sister Pamela was a Mantua maker, in other words a dressmaker. In those days before sewing machines this was an important job as all clothes had to be stitched by hand. One of Pamela's work mates was Eliza Brown and they became close friends. Nathaniel met Eliza and liked her and found out that her father was a plasterer, a very respectable man and that they lived at Bemerton on the edge of Salisbury.

They started to walk out together and Nathaniel's feelings for Eliza increased. He hesitated for some time but eventually wrote to Eliza.

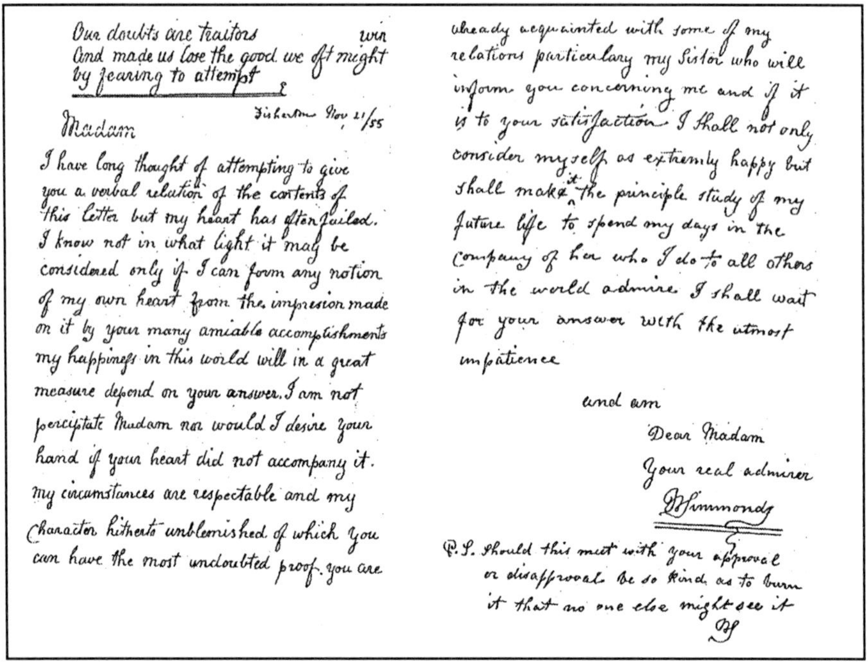

'Our doubts are traitors and made us lose the good we oft might win by _fearing to attempt_'

Fisherton Nov 21st /1855.

Madam

I have long thought of attempting to give you a verbal relation of the contents of this letter but my heart has often failed. I know not in what light it may be considered only if I can form any notion of my own heart from the impression made on it by your many amiable accomplishments. My happiness in this world will in a great measure depend on your answer. I am not percipitate madam nor would I desire your hand if your heart did not accompany it. My circumstances are respectable and my character hitherto unblemished of which you can have the most undoubted proof. You are already acquainted with some of my relations, particularly my sister who will inform you concerning me and if it is to your satisfaction I shall not only consider myself extremely happy, but shall make it the principle study of my future life to spend my days in the company of her who I do to all others in the world admire.

I shall wait for your answer with the utmost impatience.
and am Dear Madam your real admirer
N. Simmonds.

24

P.S. Should this meet with your approval or disapproval be so kind as to burn it so that no one else might see it. N. S."

Eliza said, "Yes" to Nathaniel but she did not burn the letter. She gave it to her granddaughter Edith, so we still have it in the family.

Edward and Anne Brown nee Napier

Eliza's ancestry is quite interesting. Eliza's father Edward Brown came from Westbury in Wiltshire and he comes from a long line of Browns in Westbury and earlier in Trowbridge all respectable trades people. Eliza's mother was Anne Catherine Napier, daughter of Thomas Tregenwell Napier and his wife Martha Gorringe-Troake.

Thomas's father was Rev. Edward Napier whose family goes back in Tintinhall in Somerset to the earliest Parish Registers. Thomas's mother was Anna Catherina Tregonwell of Anderson and Milton Abbey in Dorset.

I had found Thomas Tregonwell Napier's baptism, not long before we had a holiday in Bournemouth with our youngest daughter Catherine who was born in 1982. She was about eight years old and had broken her wrist so could not do much bathing as she had to keep her plaster dry! We were trying to find things to amuse her and someone said that there were squirrels in the churchyard. Catherine was happily feeding the squirrels with nuts when I noticed a large table tomb with brass plates on the sides and the name was Tregonwell, so I copied down the inscriptions.

'SACRED TO THE MEMORY OF LEWIS DYMOKE GROVESNOR TREGONWELL ESQ. OF ANDERSON AND CRANBOURNE LODGE IN DORSET WHO DEPARTED THIS LIFE AT THE LATTER OF THESE RESIDENCES ON 18 JANUARY MDCCCXXXII AGED 73 YEARS. ALSO OF GROVESNOR PORTMAN TREGONWELL HIS SON WHO DIED AN INFANT ON 29 MAY MDCCCVII. THEIR REMAINS WERE REMOVED FROM ANDERSON TO THIS SPOT ON 26 FEBRUARY MDCCCXLVI.

BOURNEMOUTH WHICH MR TREGONWELL WAS THE FIRST TO BRING INTO NOTICE AS A WATERING PLACE BY ERECTING A MANSION FOR HIS OWN OCCUPATION HAVING BEEN HIS FAVOURITE RETREAT FOR MANY YEARS BEFORE HIS DEATH.'

The memorial lists several other members of his family. At the time I did not know they were related to our family but later when I found more of Eliza Brown's ancestors I realised that Lewis D. G. Tregonwell the founder of Bournemouth was Anne Brown's great, great uncle.

The earliest Tregonwell of that family came from Cornwall. He was Sir John Tregonwell who had the job of valuing the property of the monasteries in Dorset and Somerset when Henry VIII dissolved the monasteries, at the reformation. He was given Milton Abbey to live in as his reward.

Nathaniel Simmonds and Eliza Brown were married on 26th Dec 1859 in Bemerton Chapel on the edge of Salisbury, near her parents' home. Nathaniel and Eliza had three children: another Nathaniel born in 1860, Eliza in 1862 and Henry born in 1865. They soon grew up and the younger son Henry followed his father into the leather trade & married before his elder brother. Henry married a cousin Mattie Elizabeth Brown in 1895. She was the daughter of one of Eliza's brothers, Edwin Lewis Brown who had six boys and three girls in his family. Henry and Mattie had two children: Christina Katherine and Henry Walter.

Eliza Simmonds married another Nathaniel whose surname was Sanger, in 1883. Nathaniel Sanger was a watchmaker, they had a family of four children: two boys and two girls.

The eldest Nathaniel Edward Sanger was born in 1884, he married Rose Page and they had three children, Ivor in 1911, Marcelle in 1913 and Peter in 1915. The second child Marion Sanger died as a small girl. George Wynne Sanger died in 1958 never having married. Mary Helen Sanger, born in 1900, married Harold Arthur Freeman in 1921 and died in 1933.

The following year Harold Freeman married his wife's niece Marcelle Sanger and I am in touch with their family.

The younger Nathaniel Simmonds started in his father's trade as currier but he did not like it at all; he was much more inclined to books and reading. He was also artistic as we have a certificate that reads:

"Science and Art Department of the Committee of Council of Education.
Art Students Certificate.
I hereby certify that Nathaniel Simmonds   Has passed a satisfactory examination in Freehand Drawing, Practical Geometry, Linear Perspective,
Model Drawing Of the Second Grade.
Signed H. T. Bowler
Assistant Director for Art Certificate granted 28th day of September 1880.
By order of the Committee of Council for education.   No. 9833"

Ellen and Edith Fanny Harrison

Nathaniel started to walk out with Edith Fanny Harrison the eldest of the first set of twins born to Joseph the chemist. Edith encouraged Nathaniel in his dream of having a bookshop of his own. He spent time in London learning the trade and eventually was able to open his own bookshop in Wilton Road, Salisbury. Nathaniel Simmonds married Edith Fanny Harrison on 25 January 1899.

The local newspaper headline was *'Pretty Wedding at Fisherton.*

On Wednesday a pretty wedding took place at St. Paul's church Fisherton. The weather which was delightful was most suitable to the occasion. The contracting parties were Mr. Nathaniel Simmonds eldest son of Mr. Nathaniel Simmonds of this city and Miss Edith Fanny Harrison third daughter of the late Mr J. P. Harrison also of Salisbury. The ceremony was conducted by the Revd E. N. Thwaites (Rector), aided by Revd T. H. Bland.

The Bride who was given away by her brother Mr Frederick Joseph Harrison was attired in a becoming dress of silver grey silk with a Trawlawney hat trimmed with

27

feathers to match. She also wore a lovely Maltese lace fichue the present of her brother residing in Malta.

Her three sisters the Misses Annie, Nellie and Alice Harrison were her bridesmaids. They wore cream cashmere dresses with cream pink chiffon fichues and chiffon hats to match. They also carried bouquets and wore handsome gold brooches. Bouquets and brooches were the gifts of the bridegroom. He was accompanied by Mr. Sainsbury, who officiated as Best Man. When the ceremony was concluded the small procession wended it way along the church path to the carriages. Considerable interest was manifested in the ceremony and not a little favourable comment was passed among the onlookers upon the pretty group.

Later in the day Mr. & Mrs Simmonds left Salisbury for Oxford, where the honeymoon will be spent. They were the recipients of a large number of handsome presents. Herring & Co Fisherton Mews supplied the carriages'

On the marriage certificate the witnesses who signed with the Bride & Groom are William Hy Sainsbury and Annie Eliza Harrison. Nathaniel was 38 and Edith Fanny 30 years old on their wedding day. The clergyman who officiated at the wedding was Rev. E. N. Thwaites who had baptised Edith's little brother, Richard.

Edith's father, Joseph, had died in 1894 and Frederick, her eldest brother was now running the chemist shop. The wedding was held on a Wednesday afternoon, early closing day, so that Edith's brother Frederick could come to the service and give her away.

4   The Family over the Shop at Mitre House

Edith Fanny and her new husband lived in Wilton Road at first. It was here that their first child, Edith Simmonds, was born on 17 November 1899. However, soon after this Nathaniel was able to move both the bookshop and his family into Mitre House, on the corner of New Street and High Street, just outside the Cathedral close.

Mitre House, High Street, Salisbury showing the bookshop.

This old print shows the bookshop on the corner. Harrison (when grown up) saw a tiny reproduction of the print in a magazine advert for an auctioneer. He contacted the auctioneer but the print had been sold. However Michael got a friend to photograph the tiny advert and blow up the print and the detail in it is amazing. It shows clearly the Mitre painted on the wall and the rows of books in the case on the corner.

Mitre House is a medieval building with a Bishop's Mitre painted on the wall outside. Mitre House is said to have been built for the Bishop of Salisbury to live in, while the Cathedral and city were being built in the 13th century. This is why, when a new Bishop of Salisbury is appointed, he comes to put on his robes in Mitre House. He then processes through the gateway into the Cathedral Close and knocks with his crosier at the Cathedral door, to be admitted for the first time as Bishop of Salisbury and enthroned in the Cathedral. Tradition says he leaves a five-pound note on the table in Mitre House.

Alice Harrison's Wedding 1900. Back row: Nathaniel Simmonds, Ellen, Annie, Edgar, Catherine, Embo & Ernest Harrison.
In front: Edith Fanny Simmonds with little Edith, Emily Harrison, Albert Burden, Alice Burden nee Harrison, Frederick Joseph with Marjorie and Mary Agnes Harrison.

Edith's sister, Alice, was married to Albert Burden on 29 August 1900. In their wedding group we have our only photograph of Nathaniel Simmonds. Nathaniel is standing on the left behind Edith who has little Edith on her lap. It is quite likely that Edith Fanny is wearing her wedding dress for her sister's wedding. At the back of the group on the other side is Ernest Harrison, Alice's twin, and his wife Embo, who will play a prominent part in our story later.

After little Edith, born 1899, Nathaniel & Edith Fanny had a son, Nathaniel Harrison Simmonds who was born on 9 December 1900. He was always called Harrison in the family and was very proud of the fact that he had been born in Mitre House.

Nathaniel was now in his element. He sold maps, prints and books on local history. He also ran a lending library. Some of the titles were 'Kim' by Rudyard Kipling, 'The Alien' by Montessori, 'Cardigan' by Chambers, 'The Secret Orchard' by Castle, 'Life of R. L. Stevenson' and 'In a North country village' by M. E. Francis.

In January 1901 from his cash book he had:- Cash in Bank £1 6s 0d, Cash in hand, £5 2s 9d, New books sold, £1 2s 0d, Library rents, 12s 6d, Coal, £1 1s 6d, Paid to Hutchinson (New books) 4 shillings, Paid to Brown's for second-hand books 4s 2d. On another day he sold new books for 11 s 4d and received £1 6s 0d on account and had 3s 6d for library rents. He paid £1 6s 3d income tax. How times have changed!

In the 1901 census that April the family is listed at '77 New Street, Salisbury', Nathaniel is described as 'Book and Print seller, Head, 40, working on his own account' Edith Fanny is 'Wife 32, with 'Edith dau. 1, and Nathaniel H. aged 3 months.' Also listed is 'Mary Bailey, age 16, general domestic servant.'

In the same census at 19 Rollestone Street, Salisbury, are 'Emily Harrison, Head, Widow 70 living on own means', with her daughters 'Catherine E. Harrison, 39 School Mistress, Annie E. 35 and Ellen 32' (neither given an occupation) and 'Edgar J Harrison, son 26 a cabinetmaker.'

In the Kelly's Directory of Salisbury the various family businesses are listed,
'Brown Bros. Builders merchants, 24 Castle St. & York Rd. Fisherton
Harrison J.P. & Son, Chemists, 29 Fisherton St. & London Road
Harrison Alice (Miss) Costumier, 45 Endless St.
Harrison Cath. Emily (Miss) Girls School 19 Rollestone St.
Harrison Edgar John, Cabinetmaker, 42 High St.

Simmonds N. & Co. Curriers, 33 Castle Street
Simmonds Nathaniel Bookseller Mitre House 37 High Street.'
There seems to be a bit of confusion in the various documents as to whether Mitre House was in the High Street or in New Street but as it is on the corner it is in both.

Nathaniel and Edith Fanny soon had two more daughters Ellen born 12th March 1902 and Mary born 26 March 1904 and they were a happy and contented family growing up with lots of attention from Grandparents, Aunts and Uncles and a father who loved to tell them of books and animals.

Nathaniel's mother Eliza came to live with the family after the death of her husband the first Nathaniel Simmonds who died on 9 November 1904 aged 70 years. He was buried in the Devizes Road Cemetery.

Eliza Simmonds nee Brown

We visited Salisbury with little Edith (whom we always called Aunt Ede) when she was nearly ninety. It was when Mitre House had a cafe upstairs.

Aunt Ede was thrilled to be having tea in the room where she had lived as a small child.

It had been the family's living room with windows looking both down the High street and across the High Street towards Fisherton St.

When the waitress realised that Aunt Ede had lived there as a child, Ede was allowed to look into the various doorways and she was saying, 'That is where our parents slept and that was Grandma's room and this was our room etc.'

It was a very happy day. Michael & I also were pleased to have seen the place where his father had been so happy.

This photograph of the four Simmonds children shows Edith standing beside Mary in a high chair, Harrison with the wheelbarrow full of flowers and Ellen holding the handle of a doll's pram, but whether they were their own toys or those of the photographer I do not know.

In Harrison's bedroom hung a print of a scene from the prophet Isaiah in the bible showing a lion, a lamb and a calf with a little child to lead them. We still have this picture.

We also have a scrapbook that was given to Harrison by his father. Inside the front cover is written in beautiful handwriting *'Nathaniel Harrison Simmonds from his dear Dadda Aug. 31 1904.'* There are many pictures pasted into the book, some obviously from leaflets advertising books showing book illustrations, some are postcards and some from magazines or papers. There are lots of pictures of animals and fish and quite a lot of advertisements such as one showing a typical Edwardian lady showing a bare shoulder advertising Plantol soap with a quotation *'As morning roses newly washed with dew'* from Shakespeare's 'The Taming of the Shrew.'

Edith Fanny was expecting her fifth child in 1906 when tragedy struck. In August her husband Nathaniel was taken ill with 'Gastritis.' He was in bed for two weeks and appeared to be improving and then unexpectedly he collapsed and died on 21st. August 1906 aged only 46 years old. On his death certificate the cause of death is given as 'Gastritis 14 days, Cardiac failure, certified by Frederic Vicars. M D'

From the local Paper: -

'The death of Mr Nathaniel Simmonds bookseller of Mitre House, High Street, which took place on Tuesday at the early age of 46, will come as a shock to his many friends and clients who have been accustomed to frequent his shop for supplies of their literary wants. He was known as an ardent lover of books a collector as well as a seller both of prints and rare specimens of literature. In this respect his position was unique in the city and his death will be a great loss to all who were accustomed to find in him a congenial spirit ever ready to impart or receive information of an interesting character.

Mr. Simmonds had only been ill for a fortnight and within two days of his death appeared to be recovering, so the final collapse was a great blow to his family and friends, especially to his wife who is left with four little children to mourn his death. She will receive in her trial the deep sympathy of all to whom she and her late husband were known.

Mr Simmonds was associated from early days with the Congregational Church in Fisherton and was for many years a worker in connection with its various institutions. For some time he was secretary of the Sunday School and did good service in this office. He was also most helpful in the literary Society associated with the Church and took a deep interest in the various subjects arranged for study, notably those relating to great authors, when his knowledge was always placed at the service of his friends.

From his boyhood he was a collector and lover of books, and although associated with his father in the leather business, he more then once made an attempt to start a bookshop to enable him to gratify his personal tastes and desires. He seemed to have found just the niche he was designed to fill when he took possession of the old house at Mitre Corner and filled it with a selection of old and modern literature, as well as prints, the latter specially relating to Wiltshire and the surrounding counties, to gratify the tastes of his numerous customers, and there was every prospect of his having a successful career, but he has been removed, to many as it seems, all to soon, when there was an urgent need of his presence for the sake of his wife and family, as well as for the city, for it will be very difficult to fill the gap that his departure has caused.'

The paper carried on for another three paragraphs detailing the funeral, the floral tributes and all the people who attended. It ended by saying:- '*The funeral arrangements were carried out by Mr Edgar Harrison of High Street.*' This was Edith Fanny's youngest brother, who was now an undertaker as well as a cabinetmaker and with the rest of the family, was a great support to her in the difficult times ahead.

Nathaniel Simmonds was buried in the Devises Road cemetery near his father. He left a will dated February 1904 in which he left everything to Edith Fanny and it was witnessed by Ellen and Catherine Emily Harrison.

In the late 1970's Michael & I with our children had a Youth Hostel holiday in Salisbury and we found the graves and the children did crayon rubbings of the inscriptions. Nathaniel's reads, '*IN LOVING MEMORY OF NATHANIEL SIMMONDS, BORN OCT. 17 1867, DIED AUG 21 1906. THY WILL BE DONE.*' There is a mistake on the stone as he was actually born in 1860 not 1867! (Maybe the chisel slipped!)

The other tombstone reads '*IN LOVING MEMORY OF NATHANIEL SIMMONDS WHO DIED NOVEMBER 9TH 1904, AGED 70 YEARS. ALSO OF ELIZA WIFE OF ABOVE WHO DIED APRIL 18TH 1908, AGED 68 YEARS.*'

After her son Nathaniel Simmonds died, Eliza went to live with her daughter Eliza who was married to Nathaniel Sanger. They lived at Porton outside Salisbury. We have a copy of Eliza's will. She left her estate "to be equally divided between my daughter Eliza Sanger, my son Henry Simmonds and Edith Fanny Simmonds, widow of my son Nathaniel Simmonds." She appointed Henry to be executor.

We have the bill for her funeral:-

E. J. Harrison Cabinet Maker, Upholsterer and Undertaker
May 1st 1908
To Funeral of the late Mrs Eliza Simmonds.
Superior polished elm coffin, lined and padded with mattress and pillows, side sheets and frills inside.
Fitted with brass furniture, breast plate written black.
Together with journey to Porton for measurements.
Journey to Porton for delivery of coffin.
Hearse and pair horses to Porton and back to cemetery.

4 Bearers and attendance.
Half an hours Tolling Bell, Fisherton Church.
All burial fees complete. £ 11.10.6.'
The bill was paid on 18th May 1908, by Henry Simmonds.

It seems likely that Nathaniel Simmonds' funeral two years earlier would have been very similar.

Eliza had owned three cottages in Gorringe Road and Henry sold them as part of the estate. He recieved £252.6.7 for them from Messrs. Powning, Jonas & Parker.

We also have a receipt written on notepaper headed

'H. SIMMONDS.

BOOK AND PRINT SELLER. CIRCULATING LIBRARY.

MITRE HOUSE, HIGH STREET, SALISBURY.

Received of H. Simmonds £102 4s 8d being share due to Edith Fanny Simmonds from Mrs Eliza's estate, less £1 0s 0d left to meet incidental expenses.

  Signed Ellen Harrison 31 July 08'

Ellen must have signed for her twin as by this time Edith had gone away to earn her living.

Also note that by 1908 Henry Simmonds had taken over his brother's bookshop, with Edith Fanny's approval.

Edith Fanny Simmonds was aged 37 and seven months pregnant with her fifth child when her husband died so she had to get in a manager, Mr.Latrille to run the bookshop. Edith had to split up the family and earn her own living. No widow's pensions or children's allowances in those days.

Within weeks of Nathaniel's death the family was looking for places where the children could be looked after and educated while Edith Fanny earned her living. It may have been her brother Frank Inigo (who had become a clergyman) who suggested that The Infant Orphan Asylum at Wanstead might take the younger children.

This institution had been founded in 1820 and was later known as Wanstead School. I was in touch with the archivist of the Wanstead School Trust, Marianne Thorne and she has given me details of the forms that were filled in for the children, as they were put forward to be admitted to the school.

The school was founded by Andrew Reed early in the 1820's and was for 'the children of distressed gentlefolk' They had to be orphan children of military or professional people, clergy or respectable tradespeople. There was a system by which a child was proposed (usually by a clergyman known to the family) and the child had to get 1000 votes from people who supported the charity and family members could canvas for votes.

The first child to be admitted from the Simmonds family was Ellen and I show the form as it was filled in about her.

'1. **Name of child** *Ellen Simmonds*

2. **Date of birth** *12th. March 1902*

3 **Residence** *Mitre House, High Street Salisbury (Mother)*
(Communicate with Rev. F.I.Harrison 74 Gayville Road, London SW)

4 **Christian names of parents**   *Nathaniel and Edith Fanny*
                  Maiden name *Harrison*

5 **Are both dead** *Father only.*

6 **Father's station** *High class Bookseller & Picture dealer.*

7 **Annual income of father** *Uncertain, but was always sufficient to enable the family to live very comfortably.*

8 **Cause of his death and age.** *Gastritis & Cardiac failure   46 years*

9 **Number of children now left, names and ages.** *Edith 6, Nathaniel 5 Ellen 4, Mary 2, A posthumous birth expected.*
      *(A boy born 21. 10.06 * Rev Harrison 23.10.06)*

10 How many unprovided for?   *Four*
11 Description of school attended   *Home tuition only*
12 Any disqualification by disease   *No.*
13 Any Assistance from Relatives? *Will help towards education of*
two eldest.
14 Any property remaining or expected?   *No.*
15 How are the family now supported? *At present by carrying on the*
father's business.
16 By whom nominated *C.L.S. Sanctuary, The Close, Salisbury,*
G.H. Bourne, The College Salisbury.
17 Date recieved *24ᵗʰ September 1906.*
18. If Accepted and when *27ᵗʰ September 1906*
19 If Elected or presented *29ᵗʰ November 1906 (presented erased)*
20 When admitted   *23ʳᵈ January 1907*
21 Sureties *F. J. Harrison (Uncle) 29 Fisherton Street, Salisbury. Chemist.*
H. Simmonds (Uncle) 67 Devizes Road, Salisbury. Leather merchant.
F. I. Harrison (Uncle) 74 Gayville Road, Battersea. Clergyman
22 Date of quitting *18ᵗʰ. May 1917'*

Note the date of acceptance above is barely a month from Nathaniel's death. The two nominators were both prominent clergy in Salisbury who would have known the Harrison and Simmonds families well. The form also shows Certificate details of Ellen's baptism, 18 May 1902, birth, and of Ellen's health. She was examined by W. W. Ord MD, on 20 September 1906, less then three weeks after her father's death.

The next form shows details as before of the child and where it asks about Whooping cough and Measles, Ellen had suffered both. Then the form shows details of the Father and here it *says 'Book and Print seller and Picture dealer, was often consulted and highly paid as an expert.'* His income is given as *'£300 p.a. at least.'*

Next are details of the Mother

'1 Is she still a widow? *Yes,*   **2. Has she good health** *Yes*
3 How is she employed? *Not at present, she is expecting a posthumous birth.*
4 Number of children dependent on her   *All.*
5 Character of their education *Elder children had Nursery Governess.*
6 Her relations, If able to assist *Her father was in business as a Chemist, one brother is carrying on this business; another a clergyman; others are in business and can only help temporarily*
Of The Circumstances.
1 Any property belonging to the family *No*

2 Any likely to come and when?   *No*
3 How are the family now supported *At present by takings of business and help of relatives; the business however will be disposed of.*
4 If in business what are the proceeds? *Very little now.*
5 Parochial Relief, any recieved?   *No'*

The baby, Christopher, was born on October 21st 1906 two months to the day after his father's death. It must have been a bittersweet time for Edith Fanny to have a new son and know that he would never know his father. As before she had great support from her family during this lying in period.

In January 1907 Ellen was the first of the family to leave home and go away to school aged only four years and six months. To the end of her life Ellen hated talking about those school days and she had obviously felt the separation from her family very deeply.

The forms about Mary and Christopher are almost the same as Ellen's except for some significant details.

'Number of children, 4   *2 Eldest now at Watford, 1 at Wanstead.*
How are they supported? *Mother is now Matron of Princess Mary's Village Homes, Addlestone.*
By whom nominated?   *H.C. Latrille 5 Bloomsbury Park, W. C. Rev A. G. Ward 58 Bolingbroke Rd S W'*

Was this Mr Latrille the one who had been manager in the shop I wonder? It is not a common name. The Rev Ward was probably a friend of Rev Frank I. Harrison as he lived near him. Mary was elected on 17 May 1909 and admitted to the school on 30 July 1909 aged 4 years and eleven months. Under **Any assistance from relatives** it states' *Mother's brother is keeping this child'* Her sureties were her uncles *F. J. Harrison Chemist, F. I. Harrison Curate & E. Harrison 260 Seven Sisters Road, N. (Jeweller) Uncle.*

Christopher, the new baby, at first went with his mother to Princess Mary's Village Homes and was admitted to Wanstead Infant Orphan Asylum aged 2 years and 5 months on 18 December 1909 only six months after Mary. This is according to the information on the form but by my reckoning in Dec 1909 he would have been 3 years and two months. I think the ages on the forms must be when the child was first examined and not the age when actually admitted.

Chris's Sureties are *R. S. Harrison Jeweller (Uncle), E Harrison watchmaker (Uncle) and H. Simmonds High Street Salisbury Bookseller (Uncle.)* Again it was Edith Fanny's brothers and brother-in-law who were helping her in every way they could.

39

Edith, Harrison, Edith Fanny, Mary, Christopher, & Ellen Simmonds

This photo of Edith with the children must have been taken after Ellen was at school. She hated it as all her hair had been cut off at school. Maybe she had caught scabies or nits from other children?

Within a year of her husband's death, Edith found the new manager had not the talent for the job, so he was dismissed and she handed over the bookshop to her husband's brother Henry Simmonds. Henry ran it for years and after a few years the business moved out of Mitre House to premises further down the High Street.

Henry was later joined in the bookshop business by his children, Henry Walter and Christina Katherine. They continued to run the bookshop together, right up to the late 1960s. Neither of them had married and they both died suddenly, Christina on 27 March and Henry on 16 April 1968 within a few weeks of each other so the shop had to be sold.

I remember the talk of the legacy that Nathaniel Harrison Simmonds inherited as his share of their estate after the bookshop was closed.

In 1907 Edith Fanny had gone to work as a matron at "Princess Mary's Village Homes" where she could take the new baby with her. At the Surrey History Centre in Woking I asked to look at the records of Princess Mary's Village homes but most of them are closed until 75 years after the last entry.

However I looked through a printed Annual report and although it lists all the benefactors and people who held bazaar's etc to raise funds it does not give lists of staff names. However in this rather poor photo of the staff of 1909 there is a lady who looks like Edith Fanny Simmonds. She is wearing a cap, as are several others of the staff, and is standing third from the right of the picture.

Where it says 'Staff' the list is as follows
'Superintendent Miss Wilkinson, Assistant Superintendent Miss M. Wilkinson, 4 School teachers, 4 Assistant Teachers, Nurse, Relief Nurse, Storekeeper, Sewing Matron, Dressmaker, Laundry Matron, Assistant Laundry Matron, Training Home Matron, 2 Clerks, Shaftsbury House Matron, Infirmary Mother, 10 Cottage Mothers, Chaplain, Organist & Choirmaster, Drill Instructor and Cookery Mistress.'

There are ten ladies seated without caps so I presume they are the 'Mothers.' As Edith Fanny had been trained as a court dressmaker she may well have been either the 'Sewing Matron' or the 'Dressmaker.'

However the evidence from Wanstead school records describes her as a "Matron of Princess Mary's Village Homes" so she was definitely there.

In a Directory of Surrey for 1913 I found the following description of the homes in Addlestone.

'The Princess Mary's Village Homes, of which her Majesty the Queen is patroness, were erected in 1871 & consist of a number of rough cast cottages, the central building forming a school house with a clock tower. The Institution is certified by the Home Office and London County Council, for the reception of female children of prisoners and other children in destitute or dangerous circumstances. The buildings are designed to carry out the "Family System" whereby each cottage contains a number of children under a "Mother." Accomodation for about 260 children plus holiday homes for another 15 girls. Children are admitted as infants and maintained until age 16, on payment of the maintenance charge. It includes an industrial Girls school.'

Later Edith Fanny spent some time housekeeping for her brother Frederick, first when his wife was ill and then after she died. Mary Agnes died on 19 January 1917 and her husband Frederick Joseph died on 4 October 1917 without having proved his wife's will. Edith Fanny then had to find another job. Family tradition says that she worked at Wandsworth Patriotic School for a while so it may have been at this time between 1917 and 1922 that she was there.

In 1922 she became "Matron in charge of sanatorium" at Wellington College near Sandhurst. Edith Fanny is listed in the Wellington College registers as "Miss Symonds". In those days nurses were rarely married women and it may not have been known at the college that she was a widow. Miss Symonds is listed in the registers from 1922 to 1948 when Edith Fanny was nearly eighty!

Little Edith Simmonds had an autograph book and it includes writings and pictures by several relations. A poem written in by her mother reads - *'There is so much good in the worst of us, There is so much bad in the best of us,*
That it little behoves any of us, To speak ill of the rest of us
E. F. Simmonds April 17ᵗʰ 1912'.

Little Edith had already been at school with her Aunty Cathy, but after her father's death, she was elected for a place at the orphanage school at Watford, called the London Orphan Asylum, later renamed Reed's School, as it had also been founded by Andrew Reed. The system was very similar to that of the Wanstead School for admission by voting. No children were admitted who were illegitimate or whose parents had separated. Harrison was also elected to the same school a year later.

Back row Christopher, Edith, Nathaniel H.
Front row Mary, Edith Fanny & Ellen Simmonds
about 1915

This photo taken about 1915 shows the family. At the back are Christopher, Edith and Harrison.

Seated in front are Mary, Edith Fanny and Ellen.

This was about the time Harrison left school. I was able to look at the old registers and Trustee's reports from Reed's school at the Surrey History Centre at Woking.

In the Annual Reports they each have an entry: - the girls list shows *'Simmonds Edith born 17th Nov. 1899. Admitted June 1908. Father was a Master Bookseller. 5 children dependent on mother. Salisbury'*

The boy's list is similar: - *'Simmonds Nathaniel Harrison born 9th December 1900. Admitted Jan. 1909. Father Master Bookseller. 5 children, one admitted 3 dependent on Mother. Salisbury.'*

The boys and girls were kept separate and so Harrison was only allowed to see his sister on visiting days. They would sometimes glimpse each other across the enormous dining room, but were not allowed to speak to each other. Aunt Ede said the food was quite good and there was plenty of it but she missed her family.

I found the following entry in the girl's section of the leaving register for 1893-1924.

'2372 Simmonds Edith Age 14 on 17th November 1913, dismissed 15 March 1917, to her Mother's care.'

In the boy's section of the same register is:-

'4632 Simmonds Nathaniel H. 14 years of age on 9 Dec. 1914, dismissed 16 Dec. 1915. to care of Friends.

The 'friends' were his uncle Ernie Harrison and Aunt Embo.

The 1917 issue of the London Orphan Asylum Girls Magazine includes items about those leaving.

'Edith Simmonds received the Archbishop's prize for seniors in Religious Education. She was 1st. Lieutenant of Snowdrop House and became a prefect between 1916-1917. She passed Cambridge Junior exam in 1914 and Senior Cambridge exam in 1916.'

A later magazine has 'Old Girls information:-

'Edith Simmonds 174 Regents Park Road, Chalk Farm. Now is junior clerk at Messrs Charles Comins & Co Chartered Accountants 50 Cannon Street. E.C.'

After her training Edith Simmonds (known as Ede in the family) became a governess to two small girls and went out to the Azores with the family. She learned to speak fluent Portuguese and Spanish. Edith celebrated her twenty-first birthday in the Azores.

When she returned she did a secretarial course and got a job as secretary/accountant to a man called Frank Mousley. He was a married man with two sons and a daughter, who ran a firm that made powder puffs and tennis racquets. Frank had a house and large grounds with tennis courts in East Sheen, not far from Wimbledon and he became friends with Dan Maskell the professional tennis player and later commentator. It was Frank, according to Aunt Ede, who suggested they should hold tournaments at Wimbledon and the first matches were played on Frank's courts.

I quote from Dan Maskell's book 'From where I Sit.' This was when Dan Maskell was a young man of eighteen working at Queens Club. He was playing with some of the top players of the day and wanted more matches. He says

'Accordingly it continued to frustrate me that there was so little opportunity for match play. One day I was approached by a Mr Frank Mousley who lived a few miles from Queens in East Sheen where he owned a garage behind which were four hard tennis courts.

He was very keen on the game and asked why it was that we professionals had no official association. "Why don't you form a British Professionals Association? Then you will have a much stronger voice in the game"' he suggested. I thought about this from the point of view of our lack of competition and replied: "Mr Mousley, suppose I could get eight of our professionals to come down to your courts on a Saturday afternoon, would you be prepared to advertise the matches and let us play?" "What a good idea, of course I will." he answered.

So began some most enjoyable sessions in which several of us from Queens Club - used to arrange to be away from the club on Saturday afternoons, a quiet time for coaching when the members generally played among themselves.

Each week Mr Mousley would put up £5 and the eight of us used to put five shillings each in the kitty and we'd play a knockout singles tournament followed by some doubles. From these small beginnings sprang the idea of forming the association that Mr Mousley had suggested.

In due course the Professional Coaches Association would embrace nearly every worthwhile teacher in the country and would become affiliated to the Lawn Tennis Association.'

Soon afterwards when a new magazine backed the idea of a professional championship, Frank Mousley presented a silver cup for the winner and the first person to win it was Dan Maskell.

Edith worked for Frank Mousley for a lot of years and some years after the death of his wife he asked Edith to marry him. They were married on 1 February 1938. Edith was a year younger then her stepson Maurice! Frank and Edith had one daughter, Patricia, born in 1942 and they were very happy together.

Frank died in 1950 and Edith and Pat moved to Bedford.

Pat also went to Reed's school and her entry reads:-

'3396 Patricia Edith Mousley, 15th birthday 11- 10-56, left 26-7-57, address of mother Mrs. E. Mousley, 87 Goldington Road, Bedford.
Admitted to the school on September 18th 1951 by election 12548 votes'

In the directory of Barnes Surrey for 1933 'Mrs Simmonds' is listed as a private resident at 10 Shalstone Street, Barnes, SW 14. I knew Edith Fanny must have lived somewhere near to Richmond as there are family stories of young Christopher often going riding in Richmond Park. After leaving school Chris was working at Maple's furniture store in London.

At that time young Edith was working for Frank Mousley who lived at 'The Wilderness, Derby Road, SW 14 not far away. His son Maurice was at 65 Grovesnor Ave, just down the road.

Edith & Frank Mousley

My brother-in-law Peter remembers that *'Granny had a house in Peldon Avenue, Richmond which was demolished by a land mine during the Second World War. Later she moved to a flat in Sheen Court, Sheen.'*

Peter also remembers that Edith Fanny's eldest sister Catherine was staying with her on one of his visits to the flat.

By this time Edith Fanny's brother Frank Inigo was also not far away as he was chaplain to Hickey's Almshouses in Richmond. Later Edith Fanny moved to Bedford to live with her daughter Edith when they were both widows.

Both Mary and Ellen Simmonds trained as nurses and worked until retiring age, neither married. We still have Ellen's certificates, she trained at Hampstead General and North West London Hospital and passed the final examination on 28 June 1927. She trained as a Midwife in Birmingham. She was registered as a midwife on 20 November 1937, so she must have worked for some years as a staff nurse before doing her midwifery training.

Ellen lived and worked as a district Nurse and Midwife in Newport Pagnell and Wolverton, Bucks for many years. When Ellen retired she came to live in Bedford with her sister Edith. Ellen died in Bedford on 27 August 1985 following a stroke in December the previous year.

When she first came out of hospital after the stroke Aunt Ellen, whom we always called Aunt Nell, stayed with us for as few weeks, as it would have been too much for Ede to look after her. Aunt Nell was always very grateful for any help we could give her.

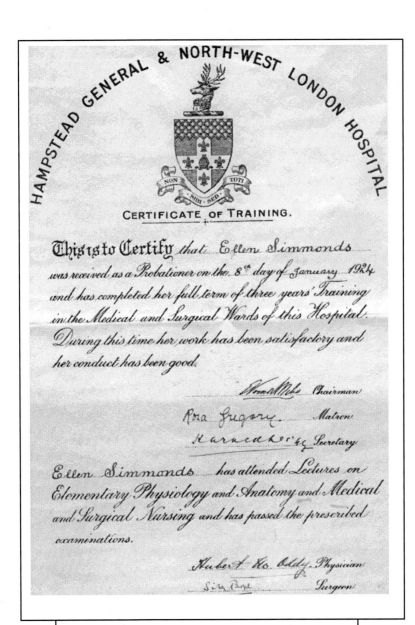

Ellen Simmonds Nursing Certificate

I remember how she used to blow a whistle for me to go down and help her if she needed to get up in the night. She had a wry sense of humour. Aunt Nell stayed with us for about six weeks until she was able to go home to her sister Ede.

Mary Simmonds also trained as a nurse at the Radcliffe Infirmary in Oxford. She also did midwifery training in Birmingham and later became an industrial nurse. We have a cutting from the 'Bristol Siddeley News' of April 1965, which tells of Mary's career.

The headline is '*She was one of the 'Bevin Girls'*'

'*I was a 'Bevin Girl' That puzzled us for a start; we had heard of 'Windmill girls', 'Tiller girls', 'Flower girls'; but 'Bevin Girls' Sister Simmonds was quick to enlighten us. ' That is how I came into industry' she told us. She was directed to Bovis Ltd., after a course in 'Industrial Nursing' where she earned the 'Bevin Girl' title applied we understand to nurses who were directed to industry for the duration of the war. She developed a liking for industrial nursing and in 1944 joined the De Havilland Engine Co., at Stonegrave, moving in 1947 to Leavesden and in 1948 to 'dear old Stag Lane' where she has been a very good friend to the hundreds of employees who have made good use of her kind help and good advice. Sister Simmonds, as you will have gathered has retired and is moving to South Wales where she will settle down with her friend by the seaside and enjoy plenty of fresh air and good country walks. She is a native of Salisbury, but has spent most of her life in the London area and was trained in nursing at the Radcliffe Infirmary and General Hospital Oxford, moving from there to Birmingham as a Queen's District nurse and then as she says she became a 'Bevin Girl'.*

She spoke of the changes in nursing since her 'training days'. At that time nurses did their studying in their off-duty hours, and nowadays extra time off is given for this purpose. Her time in hospital nursing was she said 'an era of kaolin poultices and much more strenuous than today- patients were kept in bed for longer periods than is the case these days, but the new scheme of things was undoubtedly beneficial to both patients and staff. The advances in industrial nursing had also been of great advantage to workpeople and she felt that the development of 'preventive medicine' in works surgeries had been extremely useful in keeping down the rate of absenteeism and that its further development would undoubtedly prove worthwhile. At an informal gathering in the surgery Sister Simmonds was presented with a clock, blanket, and cheque by Mr Frank Gore chairman of the Shop Stewards committee, as a token of appreciation of all his colleagues for her patience, courtesy and efficient help. Mrs Rose Martin, on behalf of the female employees, handed over a lovely bouquet to the Sister. Sister Simmonds has asked us to say that she has been extremely happy at Stag Lane and wished to thank all her many friends for their kind thoughts and good wishes.'

Ernest Bevin was the minister of labour during the war. So it was he who directed the special nursing training that Mary did. Aunt Mary was at our wedding in 1964 with her friend Elsie with whom she shared a house for many years. Mary did not enjoy her retirement for long, she suffered a heart attack and died on 26 July 1965. She had been ill for two weeks and appeared to be getting better and got up and then collapsed and died. Her illness seems to echo that of her father Nathaniel, as he also seemed to be getting better and then suddenly collapsed, so his death may well have been a heart attack.

Christopher went with his mother to Princess Mary's Village Homes. Later he went to the orphanage school at Wanstead where his sisters Ellen and Mary were also pupils. Later still when Edith Fanny was living in Richmond, Chris was with her and he used to love to go riding in the park and help look after the horses. His great friend was John Davis and they used to ride together often.

When Chris grew up he joined the Army in a Cavalry Regiment and was sent out to Egypt. There he met a nurse called Elizabeth Hesketh. They married in Egypt after the War on 17 January 1948, and had four children. Chris and Elizabeth retired to Bognor Regis and Chris died there in 1987 also from a heart attack. Elizabeth died in April 2007 and Michael, David and I attended her beautiful funeral in Bognor Regis. Her new great grandson was there with the rest of her family.

What happened to the rest of the Harrison Family?

Catherine Harrison became a teacher and ran her own school for many years, first at Rollestone Street in Salisbury, later at Cambridge House. We still have an autograph book that several of the family signed for little Edith Simmonds.

Catherine wrote '*A little thing is a little thing, but faithfulness in little things is a Very Great Thing. Catherine Emily Harrison Nov. 16th. 1911'.* Catherine died unmarried on 17th October 1949 in Salisbury.

The J.P. Harrison & Son chemist shop in 1915.

Frederick Joseph followed his father and became a chemist and later took over after his father died. He was registered with the Royal Pharmaceutical Society on 16 April 1886. His address on registration was given as Fisherton, Salisbury. He took over the business from his father and remained at that address until his death in 1917. His obituary appeared in 'The Chemist and Druggist', 'Deaths' column on October 20ᵗ 1917.

'Harrison. - At 40 Harcourt Terrace, Salisbury on October 4th, Mr Frederick Joseph Harrison, chemist and druggist aged 53. Mr Harrison succeeded his father in the businesses at Fisherton Street and London Road. He was recently elected chairman of the Wiltshire Pharmacists Association, and was a member of the Salisbury City Council and of other public bodies.'

In January 1918 details of his will were given in the same paper as follows: 'Mr.Frederick Joseph Harrison, Chemist and druggist, 29 Fisherton Street Salisbury, who died on October 4th. Left estate of the gross value of £10,739-7s 3d, of which £4,232-11s-9d is net personality. The testator left his estate to his children- Marjorie, Frederick and Josaphine - in equal shares.'

Frederick had married Mary Agnes Hunt, about 1898 and had four children, Marjorie Painter, born 1899, who later married Charles Hart. Duncan Joseph born and died 1901, Frederick George born 23 November 1902, and Josephine Emily born 12 October 1904. Josephine never married but lived all her life in the Salisbury area.

Frederick George grew up in Salisbury, until his father died when he was sixteen. George was apprenticed to a manufacturing Tobacconist in Bournemouth, where he met his future wife Beatrice Smith (known as Betty.) Later he took over a shop known as Covington's in Luton, Beds., where he became very well known in the town. He was able to buy the shop with the legacy from the Chemist's shop that had been sold after his father's death.

George and Betty had two children Joan Mary born in 1929, who married but had no children and died in 1983, and Michael Frederick born in January 1936. He became a jeweller and emigrated to New Zealand, where he married Hilary Amos in 1970. They now spend half the year in New Zealand and half in Harpenden and Michael still sells his personally made jewellery in both places.

Annie Harrison became very artistic; she painted pictures and also did carving. We have inherited a beautifully carved table that Annie carved and several of her pictures.

In Edith's autograph book Annie painted a picture of the 'Waterfall at Blair Athol, Perth Scotland', and has signed 'Annie E. Harrison Nov. 16th 1911'. Annie lived in Salisbury all her life looking after her mother until her death in 1918 and then keeping house for her sister Catherine and later living with Ellen after Catherine's death.

George Henry went into the navy where he became an engineer and later after his service was over he became involved with the manufacture of guns. George married a young widow, Annie Huxterby (nee Fowler) in July 1904 in Barrow in Furness. They had four sons Joseph Henry, born 1905, George Stanhope born 1908, Frank Benjamin born 1910 in Portsmouth and Ernest Richard born 1912 in Southsea.

George lived in Malta for some years and later in Portsmouth. Joseph Henry married May Scott and had two sons, Joseph Arthur and John Martin; both are married with two daughters each. George Stanhope married but had no children; he died in about 1975.

Frank Benjamin married Dorothy Nancy Burdett Fraser; they had a son and daughter. They have five grandchildren including three Harrisons.

Frank Inigo Harrison at first became a teacher, he married Jessica Haeber in 1894 at St. George's Battersea, but had no children. Then he entered the church and his entry in 1937 Crockford's Clerical directory reads:- " *Harrison Frank Inigo, Theological Associate of Kings College London, (1st. Class) 1901, Deacon 1901, Priest 1902 ordained by Bishop of Rochester. Curate St. Michael's Wandsworth Common 1901 to 1911, Benhilton 1911 to 1921, Vicar of Holy Trinity Barnes, 1921 to 1932, Chaplain Hickeys Almshouses Richmond from 1932. Chaplains House, Hickeys Almshouses, Sheen Road, Richmond, Surrey.*"

Frank published several religious books and wrote some beautiful Christmas poetry as well as the poem about his father's death quoted earlier.

Rev. Frank Inigo Harrison
Portrait painted by his sister Annie Eliza Harrison

The last Crockford's directory entry for him was 1949/50. His death is registered in the March quarter of 1950.

Edith Fanny and Ellen both trained as "Court Dressmakers" with the firm of Marshall & Snelgrove as did Alice also. Ellen never married; she was known as Nellie in the family. Ellen helped with the teaching at Cathy's school for sometime. In the autograph book she has painted a sketch of Salisbury Cathedral, and below it has written *'Aspire higher than to do a mean action.'* She signed *'Ellen Harrison Nov. 1911.'*

Later after Cathy died, Annie & Nellie lived together in a bay-windowed cottage in Crane Street, Salisbury. There was a long passage from the front door with a glass roof. Their distant cousins Joan and Rita French (also descended from Richard Harrison of Buckingham) remember visiting them as children. Cousin Annie was round and plump. Cousin Nellie taller and thinner. They had a clockwork mouse that they would wind up and it used to run under the piano. *'Cousin Nellie always wore a black velvet neck piece with a cameo brooch on the front'* she lived and worked in Salisbury until her death early in 1954. Annie Harrison died in the spring of 1958.

Alice Harrison married Albert Thomas Burden in August 1900 in Salisbury. Albert Burden was the founder of the Scout Motor car company, which was doing very well until the First World War. Then the government requisitioned the factory for war work and Albert never got compensation for the losses he suffered. Alice and Albert had two children Albert Ernest Burden who married and had four children and five grandchildren and Phyllis Emily Burden, born in 1906.

Phyllis Burden trained as a teacher and worked in Salisbury at first. During the Second World War she was asked if she would go to teach in Pewsey as the nearest school was in Marlborough six miles away and there was no transport and petrol rationing!

Miss Burden began her school in Pewsey in 1942 with four children. She bought three dilapidated cottages in the High Street and after some hassle from the local Authorities converted them into a school. She lived upstairs and the downstairs was the school. Soon afterwards she bought the gardens behind the buildings on each side, one a shop and one a bank, in order to have a good-sized playground for her children. Miss Burden ran the school herself until she was getting towards retiring age, when she gradually handed over to her successor.

She retired in 1970 aged 64 but continued to show interest in St.Francis School until her death aged 96, by which time the school had over 300 pupils. At Phyllis Burden's funeral the school choir sang "All things bright and beautiful" which was her favourite hymn. Phyllis called the school after St.Francis as she wanted the children to have a good role modal and St.Francis respected the wildlife and the countryside. Phyllis always had a happy school as she said, "unhappy children do not learn." Phyllis Burden taught many of the residents of Pewsey and was a well-loved personality until her death in 2002.

Ernest (Alice's twin) & Dick you will hear more of later.

Edgar Harrison, the youngest of the eleven surviving children, became an undertaker and furniture maker. Edgar had his business in the High Street near Fisherton Street where he had grown up.

This hearse was made by Albert Burden's Scout Motor Company & is outside Edgar Harrison's Undertaker's shop in Salisbury. Picture from Peter Daniels.

Edgar married Maud Cooper and they had one daughter called Margaret who went to America and was converted to the Catholic Church and later became a nun.

The family were all very close and helped each other in all things. Edgar and his brother George both died of pneumonia within two weeks. George in Malta on 28th April 1914 and Edgar on 14th May 1914 in Salisbury.

Emily Harrison has also written in her granddaughter's autograph book. The writing is very shaky and it is dated 15 November 1911.

I think it reads as follows:- '*Little duties still put off, Will end in nothing done, Bye and bye is soon enough, Has ruined many a man. Grandma.*'

Emily Harrison died at 19 Rollestone Street, Salisbury on 30th October 1918, aged 88 years of Influenza. It was her eldest daughter Catherine who registered her death. She was buried with her husband in Devizes Road Cemetery.

Back: Ernest, Alice, Richard, Ellen, Edgar, Edith Fanny, & Frank.
Front: Annie, Frederick, Emily, Catherine & George Harrison.
Probably taken for Emily's 80th birthday

In this picture the eleven children are grouped around their old mother who looks very proud of her large family. Edith Fanny is the only one standing in profile and family legend says it was because she had just had all her teeth out so could not smile!

The inscription on the tombstone reads:- 'IN LOVING MEMORY OF JOSEPH PAINTER HARRISON, AT REST OCT. 15TH. 1893, AGED 63 YEARS. ALSO OF EMILY HIS DEARLY BELOVED WIFE, AT REST OCT. 30TH. 1918 IN HER 89TH YEAR. FOREVER WITH THE LORD.'

In July 2006 my husband & I had lunch with Michael and Hilary Harrison. Michael is the son of Frederick George Harrison and grandson of Frederick Joseph Harrison. Michael showed me the original will of Joseph Painter Harrison and also of Emily Harrison and that of Mary Agnes Harrison, (wife of Frederick Joseph).

55

These documents seem to have been used as exhibits in a court case as there is written on the outside of the will of Joseph Painter Harrison thus *'Exhibit marked "EH 1" referred to in an affidavit of Ernest Harrison Sworn 22nd August 1918. High Court of Justice Chancery Division, Mr Justice Eve, 1918 H - 1041, on Harrison Trust. Harrison v. Harrison.'*

There is also a memorandum hand written on the outside
' By a conveyance dated 2nd August 1919 between Ernest Harrison & George Nicholson of the first part, Catherine Emily Harrison, Annie Eliza Harrison, Frank Inigo Harrison, Edith Fanny Simmonds, Ellen Harrison, Alice Burden, Richard Sydney Harrison, Ernest Harrison, Annie Clara Harrison, Joseph Henry Harrison, George Stanhope Harrison, Frank Benjamin Harrison, Ernest Richard Harrison, & Maud Elizabeth Harrison of the second part, & Marjorie Painter Harrison, Frederick George Harrison & Josephine Emily Harrison of the third part.

All those messuages No's 29, 31, 33, Fisherton Street Salisbury, with garden at rear & garden at side, as then occupied there with their casements and appertences belonging including the use and benefit of such right of way over and along the passage running between the premises and no 35 Fisherton Street as then existed was conveyed unto the said Marjorie Painter Harrison, Frederick George Harrison and Josephine Emily Harrison in fee simple as joint tenants and their right to production of the within written probate was given'

A 'messuage' is a legal term for a plot of land. Although I have scant knowledge of legal matters the fact that all three wills name Frederick Joseph as executor, and that he died before Emily, made it that Ernest Harrison was the one who had to sort out not only his father's and mother's wills, but also those of his brother Frederick and his sister -in-law Mary Agnes.

Then as Frederick was the legatee of the chemist shop in his father's will I presume that had to be sold and then all the wills sorted out. The list 'of the second part' seems to include all the surviving children of Joseph Painter and Emily, plus the children of the ones who had died before their mother. They all had a share in the premises in which the shop had been, but only Frederick's children had the shares in the business.

So all the aunts and uncles and cousins had to convey to Frederick's children the rights to the land before the shop could be sold to Boots the Chemist. It was this legacy that enabled George Frederick Harrison to buy his shop in Luton.

Ernest (Alice's twin) spent some years living and singing as a chorister of Salisbury Cathedral. In the 'Register of old Choristers of Salisbury Cathedral, 1810 - 1897' his entry reads: -

'Harrison Ernest; born June 24,1871; son of J.P. Harrison, 29 Fisherton Street, Salisbury; came Jan. 1881; left July 1886; Lay reader at St. Martin's Colchester, since Easter 1896; Watchmaker and Jeweller. Address 22 High Street Colchester.'

A later issue of the Registers of Chorister's School Salisbury 1810 - 1921 published 1921, gives some more details: -

'Harrison Ernest, born June 1871, came Jan 1881, left July 1886, married 1901, Jeweller 1886, in Choir of St. Ambrose Westbourne 1889 - 1901, lay reader at St.Martin's Colchester 1896-1899, Sidesman at St Paul's Church Harringay 1906, Choir treasurer & secretary St. Paul's Church Harringay 1908. Address 20 Mount Pleasant, Tunbridge Wells.'

Richard Sydney Harrison, who was always called Dick in the family, married Louise (Louie) Wright. Ernest was a great joker and the tale is told that when Dick first brought Louie home for a meal, Ernest was sitting opposite her at the table next to Dick. During the meal Ernest put his foot into Louie's lap. She thought it was Dick's foot so she began to stroke and caress the foot. After a little while Ernest said, 'If you have finished with my foot, Louie, I'll have it back!' Louie must have been a good sport as she married Dick anyway. Dick and Louie had two sons and a daughter. Dick also became a jeweller and later Ernest and Dick moved to Tunbridge Wells and set up in partnership.

Ernest Harrison married Emily Adelaide Heasman on 8th April 1901 in Colchester. She became known as Aunt Embo or Emmy, but they had no children so they adopted young Nathaniel Harrison Simmonds. He went to Reed's School in 1909 left in 1915 and spent his holidays with Uncle Ernie and Aunt Embo. Harrison started to learn the jewellery trade and, aged 15, spent some time training in Hatton Garden in London.

Then he worked for a while at Selfridges shop in Seven Sisters Road, Finsbury Park, before joining his two uncles in Tunbridge Wells. The directory of Tunbridge in 1916 shows 'Harrison E. & R. S. Jewellers at 6 Calverley Road'. Under Private residents it shows Ernest Harrison at 7 Amhurst Road, and Richard S. Harrison at 71 Upper Grosvenor Rd. Tunbridge Wells.

During the First World War, a doctor was attending to Ernest at home. Ernest happened to mention that his wife, Embo, had a little lump on her breast. The doctor examined her and decided that an operation was necessary to remove the lump. The story goes that there was an air raid by Zeppelins during the operation at their house. Also that Embo had offered to thread the needles for the stitching up! Embo made a good recovery from the operation.

Harrison enjoyed his work and was a very cheerful person who loved to tell jokes and crack puns. He got this from his Uncle Ernie who had a great reputation for being a practical joker. Ernie had a small cushion that made a rude noise as one got up from the chair after sitting on it! He also had a drinking glass with a lacy edge that dribbled the water or juice down your chin as you drank, as well as a box of matches that vibrated when you picked it up and you dropped it in surprise!

Ernie and Embo were having a party one evening and during the evening a Policeman was ushered in and asked all the guests to put on their coats and then the policeman went through all their pockets. Some of the guests were found with 'silver' in their pockets! It was a practical joke planned by Ernie!

Uncle Ernie, Nathaniel H. Simmonds & Aunt Embo in their car.

We have a small silver rose bowl that was an engraved gift to Ernest and Embo from Harrison for their silver wedding anniversary. The inscription reads: -

'To Mr.& Mrs Harrison (Uncle and Auntie) on the occasion of their Silver Wedding, in affectionate gratitude, from Harrison. 8-4-26'

Harrison did very much appreciate the love and support that he had recieved from Ernie and Embo. Harrison had grown up to be a handsome young man. He met a blonde girl whom he liked and he asked her to marry him, although his Uncle and Aunt did not think much of her. Harrison could not wait to get married and have his own home.

Then one wintry day a young lady came into the shop to have her watch repaired. Harrison was smitten at first sight and is said to have followed her later and thrown a snowball at her to attract her attention.

Harrison & Violet

She was supposed to be going out to India as a nursery governess but she decided at the last minute not to go, because she was going to get married!

Harrison jilted the other girl and soon became engaged to Violet Emily Butcher. Her parents, George Butcher and Ada Emily nee Waddington, had split up when she was still small and she had been sent to a Catholic Convent boarding school and had found the Roman Catholic faith was right for her.

Violet took the name Madeleine as her Catholic baptismal name and that is why she was known as Madeleine the rest of her life. Madeleine's Godmother on her reception into the Church was an older girl, Alice Cullen. Alice was like an extra Grandmother or Great Aunt to the young Shiners and Simmonds.

Violet's mother had gone to live in Colchester, in a house owned by her father and she died there in 1923, so the only person Violet still had close to her was her sister, Ethel, who was two years younger. Ethel had no memories of their father living with them. They were still in touch with their mother's family but not close.

Violet's mother, Ada Emily had been the eldest daughter of the six children of Thomas Flesher Waddington who was an engineer in Colchester and quite well off. Thomas was married to Elizabeth Roe who had grown up in Norwich, as had Thomas.

Thomas's father James Waddington was born in Otley in Yorkshire. Elizabeth's father was John Roe and her mother was Evangelist Tarte, who had been born in Great Yarmouth, but I think she came from a French or Belgian family.

George & Ada Butcher with Violet

Thomas had his eye on a young solicitor that he thought would suit Ada Emily. However Ada did not want to get close to the young man, so she was sent away to Reigate to work in a firm that made matching curtains, cushions etc. (All sewn by hand in those days.)

George Butcher was an ironmonger, a widower with at least one son. It is not known how they met but he was some sort of traveller in ironmongery. George later had an ironmongers shop in Woodford Green, Essex. He courted Ada Emily and she agreed to marry him. He was forty-two and she thirty-five when they married on 14th. June 1905.

Violet and Ethel were born two years apart in 1906 and 1908. They lived in Woodford but the parents were not really compatible and they separated about 1910. Ethel did not remember her father living with them at all. Ada and Ethel moved to Colchester and Violet was sent to the convent boarding school in Croyden.

We still have the 'Matriculation Certificate' that Violet recieved from 'Convent of Ladies of Mary', Croyden at Midsummer 1924 after seven years of study. The subjects Violet studied were, English Language & Literature, English & Modern European History, Geography, Religious Knowledge, French, Latin, Arithmetic, Algebra, Geometry, Numerical Trigonometry, Elementary General Science, Botany, Class singing,

Needlework, Drawing, and Physical Exercise. We have a Harmsworth's Atlas that Violet used at school with interesting details about the countries in the pages between the maps, and some very detailed maps of the First World War. So Violet was a very well educated young lady.

Wedding in Tunbridge Wells 3rd November 1926.
Back: Aunt Embo & Ernie Harrison, Ernest Burden, Edith & Edith Fanny Simmonds. Centre: Nathaniel Harrison & Madeleine Simmonds, Front: Ethel Butcher.

Harrison pondered hard about their future together and decided to be instructed in the Catholic faith and in due time he was also received into the Catholic Church.

Violet Emily Butcher and Nathaniel Harrison Simmonds were married in Tunbridge Wells Catholic Church on 3rd November 1926. Their first child Peter Ernest was born a year later on 22nd November 1927, in Tunbridge Wells and they were very happy together.

Harrison & Madeleine Simmonds visiting Uncle Dick & Aunt Louie after the War.

By this time Uncle Ernest was getting towards retiring age so he said to Harrison, 'Do you want to carry on in this business or would you rather have something different, as one of these days it will be yours?' Harrison replied that he had always thought that a tobacconist shop would be fun, as he would get to know regular customers.

They discussed the possible split with Uncle Dick who did not relish the responsibility but he soon became reconciled to the idea.

Dick and Louie had two sons John, (known as Jack) and Ernest and a daughter Mary. The directories of Tunbridge Wells show that the business became R. S. Harrison & Son. It was listed at 14 Grosvenor Road, Tunbridge Wells from 1948 right up until 1970. So Jack or Ernest must have carried on with the jewellery business after Dick retired. However Harrison and his family were still very friendly with Uncle Dick and Aunt Louie and sometimes visited them after they moved to Bedford.

So in 1927 Uncle Ernie and Harrison studied the trade magazines and found a business going for sale in Bedford. Ernest and Harrison thought it over and decided to buy it and the jewellery shop in Tunbridge Wells was handed over to Dick and his family.

The business that was being sold at 78a High Street, Bedford, had been a tobacconist's shop since 1890. Strangely enough this was called Covington's, as was Harrison's cousin George's tobacconist business in Luton. W. H. Covington had both lived and worked in the Bedford premises and in the Directory of 1914 he is shown as both a tobacconist and a toyshop.

By 1918 the premises had been divided into two with the tobacco in 78 and the toyshop now called 'C. M. Scantlebury' at 78a. In 1923 the tobacconist shop had moved into 78a and 78 was now the Carlton Shoe Company. W. H. Covington must have retired soon after as in 1926 the tobacconist shop is called 'W. P. Mayo.' It was William Percy Mayo who sold the tobacco business to Ernie Harrison and Nathaniel H. Simmonds in May 1928.

So in May 1928 the two households moved up to Bedford and founded Harrison & Simmonds. Harrison was Uncle Ernie, the senior partner and Simmonds was Nathaniel Harrison Simmonds, the junior partner. From the balance sheet on 21 May 1928 the business was worth £4,000. Ernie owned two thirds of the business and Harrison one third. At first the Shop had a shared entrance with The Carlton Shoe Co.

The premises were very small about twelve feet across and twenty feet long, with a tiny office at the back and a toilet down the yard at the back. There was a trap door in the office to a cellar under the shop, and also a tiny room above where they stored stock.

Ernie and Harrison took over a young girl called Phyllis Hayward with the business, as an assistant. Phyllis had worked for Mr Mayo in his other shop in Midland Road before coming to the High Street. Mr Mayo worked with them at first but it was Phyllis who taught the practicalities of the tobacco trade to Harrison and Ernie.

They called her 'Sunshine' because of her lovely smile. She remembered that they opened at 8 am and closed at 8 pm and the door was open all the day, regardless of the weather. They used to have posh cars stopping outside while Major this or Captain that came in for their cigars or tobacco. They would pay the bill but Phyllis had to go out and deliver the orders on foot, as 'Gentlemen did not carry parcels!' Harrison would go home for lunch and Ernie would come in to watch the shop but he did not stay long once Harrison was back. Phyllis remembered selling 20 Players at eleven and a half pence to Mr. Peacock, the auctioneer, every day.

One day an irate lady came in to the shop and complained that she had slipped on a banana skin in the entrance. Harrison told her 'Madam, you will have to complain next door! We only have right of way!'

After the first year they had made a loss of £350 that was shared by the two partners. During that time Harrison had drawn £220 to support his growing family. Many of the customers used to 'Put it on the bill' and sometimes they were not very prompt at paying the bill when it was sent! On 17 May 1930 profits drawn by E. Harrison were £203 11s 4d, profits drawn by N H Simmonds were £101 15s 8d. Total profits were £305 7s 0d. During 1930 Harrison was given an extra salary of £60 0s 0d as 'Management salary.' Phyllis's wages totalled £116 9s 0d.

Phyllis Hayward outside Harrison & Simmonds.

After two years Harrison & Simmonds opened a second small shop in St Mary's Street south of the river bridge. The agreement is dated 1 July 1930. 'Mr. H. W. Valentine and Messrs E. Harrison & N. H. Simmonds Agreement for sale of Tobacconist and Hairdressers Business and premises at 19 St. Mary's St. Bedford'. The completion date was 25 August 1930.

They received the goodwill and the fixtures and fittings for £1,200 and agreed to lease the property for 21 years at a rental of £75 per annum for the first seven years, £80 for next seven years and £85 thereafter.

This little shop was at the front of a barbershop/hairdresser, so many of the men going for a haircut or shave would buy their tobacco on their way in or out. It was at the St. Mary's shop that Harrison sold cigarettes to some of the crew of the R101 Airship the day before the ill-fated maiden flight from Cardington near Bedford to India in October 1930. He would have joined in the shock and horror of the Airship's crash and burning in France.

On 31 May 1931, Phyllis's wages totalled £141 8s 6d, the profit was £287 12s 6d which was divided between Ernie £191 15s 0d and Harrison who got £95 17s 6d. On 28 May 1932 Ernest Harrison's share of the profits was High Street £177 19s 1d and St. Mary's £28 1s 7d. Nathaniel Harrison Simmonds got £88 19s 6d from the High Street and £28 1s 8d from St. Mary's.

The new shop front 1933

In 1933 a new shop front, with a central door and two small windows was fitted to the High Street shop. It cost £205 16s 6d.

The shops sold cigars, cigarettes, pipes and tobaccos and anything connected, such as matches, lighters, cigarette boxes, ashtrays & tankards that cigars could stand in. Harrison would not sell anything that was not connected with smoking.

Each Christmas Eve, Harrison would be anxiously watching the takings as they came in and praying that they would do better then last year! If they got past the last years total by 4pm he would send Phyllis out to buy cream cakes for tea.

The family was also growing. Harrison's eldest son Peter Ernest, was six months old before they moved to Bedford. A second son John arrived on 3 June 1929, then came Mary born 30 October 1933, Michael on 21 July 1936, and finally David on 30 September 1938.

The family rented apartments in London Road and then at 16 Woburn Road but settled at 1a Clapham Road on the corner of Clarendon Street. This was where Michael and David were born and where they lived throughout the war. When Peter started school at the Holy Ghost Convent infant school, it was often Phyllis who took him to school, on her way to the shop.

One day when John was a baby Madeleine found Peter feeding him with mud! Later he had a lucky escape. John was having his hair cut by Mr Wilkinson, who had a habit of giving his small customers a boiled sweet to help them keep still. (This would be frowned on today!) Madeleine was sitting reading a magazine while she waited. She glanced up and saw that John's face was blue! She jumped up, pushed Mr Wilkinson out of the way, turned John upside down and banged him on the back and was then able to hook out the sweet from his mouth. He had almost choked to death!

Madeleine also saved Mary at one time. I will use Peter's words to describe this event. '*The memory of Mary going up in flames is still quite vivid in my mind though not all the details of course. I think it was the Daily Express that had been advertising DIY kits for large gliders for only 5/-. The wingspan must have been about 3 feet. Contrary to the usual practice for such kits, the wooden parts and materials were of spruce instead of balsa wood. The frame when completed would be covered with thin brown paper instead of tissue. The adhesive for assembly was animal glue to be heated to melt into a liquid state for use. I think our parents had ordered two of these kits for John and me, perhaps for Christmas presents one year.*

When they arrived however the construction was found to be beyond our capabilities so Mum and Dad settled down to work while we 'helped' where possible, e.g. heating the glue on the kitchen gas cooker. I think that is what we were doing, waiting for the glue to heat sufficiently while Mum & Dad were next door working on the gliders on the dining room table. I suppose John & I were doing something else while waiting for the glue to melt when I suddenly looked up and saw Mary standing on a chair beside the gas stove, reaching up for something on the shelf above. The hem of her very light summer dress must have been close to the gas ring and was already flaring before she knew anything was amiss.

I just screamed in fright, probably not thinking at all how to raise the alarm or call for help. Mum & Dad came quickly however and Dad went straight to the sink to collect water to put out the fire. Mum brought Mary down to roll her in the length of carpet in front of the Gas stove. Dad was standing on the other end of the carpet at the sink so Mum had a job to get him to take his feet off it! They then took Mary next door onto the table where they had been working. I do not think Mary suffered any scars of other ill effects of the experience. She had been rescued very promptly.

I do not remember what she had been reaching for, perhaps it was for matches which were kept above the gas stove. By the way the gliders flew well, once we managed to launch them from the Modern School field. This was a difficult process however, requiring quite a long spool of twine, rather like flying a kite. Eventually they flew away and were lost.'

Michael remembered that Mary suffered a slight burn on her thigh and carried the scar for the rest of her life.

Peter remembers a visit they made to Great Uncle Frank Inigo Harrison while staying with their Grandma in Richmond. "*Uncle Frank lived only a block or two away so John & I walked round there one day to visit him. He was extremely deaf and used a large old fashioned horn into which one spoke in an effort to communicate! I remember him as a very kind old gentleman who showed us various things of interest and gave us refreshments before we returned to Granny's.*"

Peter also remembered how John and he had pedal cars that they used to race along Woburn Road on the pavement. '*Our parents were necessarily thrifty and would themselves make toys for our Christmas presents. One year it was a set of cages for metal zoo animals of which John had already started a collection. A farm was similarly constructed, largely of plywood and everything nicely painted*

It was also at Woburn Road that we had great fun with a sand pit in the garden. I remember going with Mum to a builder's yard to order the sand. We had a number of Dinkey Toy vehicles including lorries that could traverse the series of roads formed in the sand.'

Peter also remembers '*Like Granny, Auntie and Uncle (as we usually called them) would invite John and me to spend a week or so with them, not at home but to where ever they spent their summer holiday usually at Clacton or Skegness. This was quite an experience for us as we seldom went away on holidays as a family. I do remember family holidays at Hastings and Woburn Sands. I do not know which years but think they must belong to the pre-war Woburn Rd period.*

Another memory of Peter's was when Father Wyatt, the curate, called to take Peter to the Granada cinema. Cinemas were out of bounds during school term time, but Father Wyatt wanted company so Peter went with him feeling a bit apprehensive about what would happen if caught by school prefects!

Edith Fanny Simmonds with grandchildren Peter, John & Mary.

Peter and John became collectors of moths and butterflies, helped by their Mum and with library books to help identify the various specimens. Harrison and Simmonds supplied old display cabinets for their collections.

Harrison was gaining confidence in his new trade and he began to specialise in mixing his own tobacco brands. They were known as 'In house blends.' One of the first was 'Major's Mixture' made for Commander Martin of Lansdowne Rd, who always had a carnation buttonhole and wore a monocle in his eye.

In 1936 Harrison took over half shares in the business instead of only one third, as at first. They also sold the St. Mary's business; they finished there on 28 March 1936. They had employed a manager at St Mary's who proved to be not very honest so they got rid of him and sold that shop and concentrated on the High Street business. We still have the bill dated 1st April 1936 from Conquest, Clare & Binns, Solicitors, Mill Street Bedford for the final settling of that sale. They received £500-0-0 for Goodwill, fixtures and fittings and £20 for stock taken over by Mr. W.C. Stephens.

By this time Ernie was really a sleeping partner. Aunt Embo and her sister Florence Heasman, who lived with them, also had money invested in the business. When King George VI and Queen Elizabeth were crowned in May 1937, Uncle Ernie took the boys and Mary in his car, along the embankment to see all the coloured lights and decorations. Uncle Ernie and Aunt Embo presented them with a magnificent model of the horse-drawn coronation coach and procession as a souvenir of the royal occasion.

When Phyllis left the shop to marry Reg. Bustin in 1937, she recieved a lovely letter she treasured all through the years.

'Harrison and Simmonds,
78a High Street, Bedford,   17-7-37
Dear Phyllis ,
We wish to express in a very few words our warmest appreciation of your very loyal service over the past nine and half years. We have always looked upon you as a good friend and know full well that you have felt just the same towards us.
Your future carries with it our most sincere good wishes. It gives us very great pleasure to see you entering married life with one for whom we have a great regard, knowing him to be a real good chap. We shall always watch with interest and pleasure, your progress and happiness.
We remain your very sincere friends.
E. Harrison & N. H. Simmonds'

Michael & I talked to Phyllis in 1988 and she quoted the letter by heart. She thought back with affection to all the years she had spent working with Ernie and Harrison.

Ernie Harrison died in 1938 and there was a lengthy report in the Bedfordshire Record.

'*Mr. E. HARRISON, Funeral of a Bedford Tobacconist.*

The funeral of Mr. Ernest Harrison, senior partner in the firm of Harrison and Simmonds, tobacconists, of High Street Bedford, who died at his home 1 Beresford Road, Bedford on 13th April, took place at Elstow Abbey Church yesterday (Thursday). He was sixty-six years of age and was a member of several Masonic lodges. He was also vice-president of the Wiltshiremen in London.

A cremation took place at Golders Green on Saturday. The Vicar of Elstow. The Rev. S. V. Hartley, conducted the service and he was assisted by the Rev. Frank Inigo Harrison of Richmond (Mr. Harrison's brother). The choir was in attendance and Mr. W. F. Taylor was the organist. The cremation casket was interred in the Abbey Churchyard, the Rev. F. I. Harrison officiating.

The Chief mourners were Mrs. E. A. Harrison (Widow), Mr. R. S. Harrison (brother) Mr. & Mrs N. H. Simmonds, Mr F. G. Harrison, Mr E. Burden, Miss P. Burden, Mr. C. Heasman, Mrs R. Bailey, Mr L. Wakeling and Mrs. H. Fenton (nephews and nieces) Mr and Mrs A Heasman (brother in law and sister in law) Miss F. Heasman (sister in law) Mr and Mrs. C. Wakeling (cousins) Mr J. Tinsley (old friend), Mrs. E. Dilley, Miss E. Smith and Mrs E. Hayward. (Friends.) Among those at the Church were Mr Lewis W. Neate (Worshipful master, Russell Lodge, 4413) Mr Harry Kishere (worshipful Brother, Director of ceremonies, Russell lodge, 4413) Mr Edwin J. Neate (S.W. Russell Lodge) Mr. A. B. Auber (Sir William Harpur Lodge) Mr Arthur F. Lindley (Sir William Harpur Lodge 2343). Mr J. T. Coltman (representing the Bedford tobacconists and Bedford Park Bowling Club), Mr. Frank Heath (representing the Bedford Chamber of trade) Mr. F. O. Timmins (representing Messrs. McPherson, Timmins, and Ednie), Mr E.C. Lowings (representing the Bedford Conservative Club, Mr. A. Gale, Mr. F. E. Hood, Mr. P. E. Gamman, Mr. A.A. Mummery, Mr Wallace Covington, Mrs W. H. Covington, Mr and Mrs A. V. Pryer, Mrs and Miss Bailey, The Misses K and F. Bowyer, Mrs Cartilidge, Mrs F. Heath, Mrs J.T. Coltman, Mrs & Miss Gray, Mrs A.M. Adams, Miss Adams, Mr and Mrs W. B. Edwards and Mrs C.R. Devitt.'

We still have the programme for the Funeral Service, that took place at Elstow Abbey because that was where Ernie and Embo used to worship.

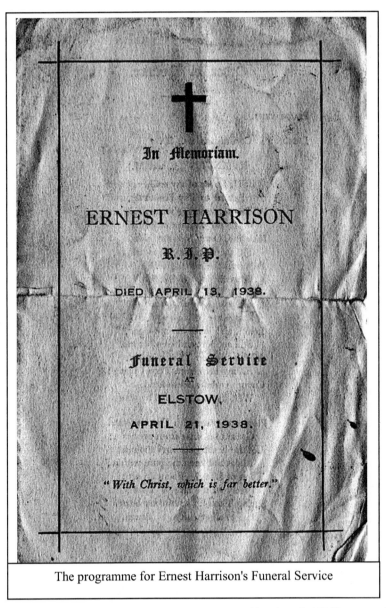

The programme for Ernest Harrison's Funeral Service

It is headed 'In Memoriam' gives '21 April 1938' etc and at the bottom says 'With Christ, which is far better.' They said Psalm XXIII and read from St.Paul I Corinthians XV, verse 20. 'It is true that Christ has been raised from the dead as the first fruits of all who have fallen asleep.' The two hymns were 'Jesu Lover of my soul' and 'Holy Father cheer our way' with 'Nunc Dimittis' at the end. The body was taken all the way to Golders Green for the cremation that was not so common in those days. Then Ernie's ashes were interred in the Elstow Churchyard, that he loved, by his brother Rev. Frank Harrison.

Harrison was now the senior partner in Harrison and Simmonds, with Embo and some other relations having money invested in the business. The total profits for the past year were £680 11s 4d. He also became an agent for the Sun Insurance Company, generously allowing his commission as discount to his clients.

When war broke out in 1939 Harrison was turned down for the Army as he had a heart murmur so he continued in the shop.

Nathaniel Harrison Simmonds in uniform. Detail from the group photo of the Observer Corps. Taken 1945.

For the duration of the war, Harrison joined the Observer Corps, where he worked shifts in the underground bunker on the corner of Days Lane, Biddenham.

This is the site where they have recently built new houses in 'Observer Close! I am told that one night after his shift, walking home in the fog and blackout, Harrison walked into a lamppost and gave himself a black eye.

In August 1939 the local papers were full of ARP rehearsals and news of evacuees coming to Bedfordshire.

One journalist wrote, *'As the warning sirens screamed their warning through a darkened Bedford, I looked into the Control Room. Nine girls were sitting beside nine telephones, while nine other telephonists sat waiting to relieve them. Beside each telephone was a red printed form with spaces to be filled in. I bent down and read: 'Air Raid Damage - position of occurrence- type of bombs- Casualties approximate number, whether any trapped under wreckage- Fire- Damage to mains- Position of unexploded bombs' Yes it was all there waiting to be filled in and no doubt the moving finger would soon be writing and having written moving on to fill in another form."*

The reporter goes on for several columns detailing all the preparations that were in hand to deal with the expected attacks from the 'Enemy.' Another reporter tells of the *"Eerie Street Scene. It was a dark forbidding town in which blue and green lights glinted eerily that I found myself in when the air raid warning sounded at ten minutes to midnight. Cars with black hoods over their headlights glided mysteriously from side-turnings and no motor vehicle showed more then its side and rear lights. As I turned into High Street from St.Paul's Square midnight chimed, the bells sounding with unnatural clamour in the dead silence that followed the warbling sirens blasts. The High Street without lights looked just like any other street and the colours of the traffic lights showed up only as tiny pinpoints of light. One shop in Silver Street had been overlooked; its lights were blazing throwing a massive beam across the road along Mill Street. At*

St.Peter's green the lights were on at the public conveniences and at the Bus shelter. As I passed the Broadway Milk Bar where the girls were just clearing up, an Air Raid Warden with his helmet on and gas mask at the ready was shouting to them to put the lights out.'

Once the lights were left on by mistake in Harrison and Simmonds and the police had to go out to find Harrison to switch them off.

In November 1939 rationing was introduced and Madeleine had to register her family for butter, bacon, ham, sugar etc at Gents in Tavistock Street and she had only to buy from that shop all through the war. There are large adverts in the papers for Dudeney and Johnston Ltd., Debenhams and various other large shops. Madeleine rented two allotments where she grew vegetables and fruit to help feed the family. She also kept rabbits to supplement the meat ration. The children soon got used to carrying a gas mask with them at all times.

Phyllis Bustin came back to work in the shop during the war. Business was not easy in wartime. Sometimes Harrison would receive an order in the morning, unpack and shelve it and he would be sold out again by evening. They would make tiny rolls of 10 cigarettes and have them all lined up so that the queue could be served quickly when the door was opened.

There was a notice in the paper in September 1941 asking all men & women born between September 1881 and September 1923 to register for Civil Defence Duties. This would be when Phyllis also joined the Observer Corps. These shifts were in addition to their full time work in the Shop.

Peter tells that *'It was important for Observer Corps staff to study and recognise allied and enemy warplanes. The same applied for the army cadets to which we belonged at school. Accordingly our whole family developed considerable skill at aircraft identification. Silhouettes were published for the purpose and we made our own epidiascope for projecting them onto a screen (usually the wall). We would then flash them one after the other and compete for correct identification. I was also a keen model maker of these war planes and used to sell some of them at school. The epidiascope was used to enlarge the silhouettes to the scale required for modelling. For this purpose the machine was rigged up in vertical position so the projected plane could be traced onto paper.'*

Michael had a little pedal car that was bought for him by Aunt Embo Harrison. He used to push it up the slope towards Manton Heights and then whizz down again. There were no houses up there then. Michael was heartbroken when on one of his rides down the slope the car axle was broken. He had great faith in his big brothers' ability to mend things and could not understand that this time they were unable to put it right. Peter made Michael a model of a Lancaster Aircraft and John made him some armoured cars. He played with them in the garden and went in and left them one night and they were taken from the garden so he was very upset. However we do still have some other models made by Peter and John.

At the end of December 1941 the Bedfordshire Times featured a page of '*Interesting Events at the Bedford Schools.*' It includes prize giving at the Carol Concert of the lower school of Bedford Modern and among the prizes given out by Mr Rowland Hill O.B.M. is '*Miss Haines's prize for French Reading, P. E. Simmonds.*' Harrison and Madeleine must have been proud of their son.

Peter remembers that the Bedford Modern School (then in Harpur Street where the Harpur shopping centre is now) was shared with another school, which was evacuated from London for safety. This meant that the Bedford boys only had the school during the mornings, and Owen's School used the premises in the afternoons.

The afternoons for the Bedford boys were filled with Cadets, sports, music in other premises and farming parties where the boys went in a lorry to a farm and helped with hoeing or pea picking etc as they were needed. The boys were paid for their work and sometimes given fruit or vegetables etc as a bonus. Peter also told us that sometimes the red glow of the burning fires in London during the blitz could be seen in the sky in Bedford. '*One of the few bombs dropped on Bedford, killed a well known citizen because he was standing outside his shelter watching the action.*' Michael says it was after the all-clear siren had sounded!

Early in the war Harrison went down to Barlings Pipes in London and bought up the old stock they had in the cellar. There were ancient silver mounted pipes and all sorts of old stock. Harrison paid them 2 s 6d for each pipe and sold them for 5s and thus was able to have a stock of pipes throughout the war when most shops could not get any more. In May 1941 for the first time the Profit was over £1,000-0-0. It was divided equally between Harrison & Mrs E. Harrison (Aunt Embo.)

There was a scheme whereby people could go into a shop and order and pay for cigarettes and tobacco products to be sent overseas to their men folk in the services. Harrison got special forms printed by 'Henry Burt & Co.' Then the wives or mothers could just fill in the amount and the brand and pay the money and Harrison would do the rest. The advertisements in the papers were for 'Players Please' and 'Navy Straight Cut' advertised as the Navy's favourite cigarette.

Old Mrs Covington still owned the shop property. Her family apparently kept her short of money. She used to ride down the High Street on her tricycle and come in and grumble to Harrison about never having any money of her own. So one day he said to her 'I will give you one hundred pounds if you will sell me the thirty years lease, with a fixed rent.' Quick as a flash Mrs Covington said, 'Done.'

Harrison advised her to go and check with her solicitor, which she did. The solicitor advised against it but 'Old Mother Covington' came back later and closed with the offer, as she wanted the money. So Harrison had the lease and a set rent of £40 four times a year, a total of £160.00 per year.

Soon after this Harrison had the opportunity to buy the premises for £8000, his bank manager was willing to lend the money, but he decided against it as he was afraid the premises might be destroyed by bombing.

When the evacuees arrived soon after the outbreak of war, the Simmonds family had a young lady called Wendy billeted on them with her baby. The family pet was a little Scottish terrier called Jock. One day Wendy left the garden gate open and Jock ran into the road and was run over by a bus.

Michael came home from school and found his mother weeping over Jock's dead body that was laid on the mat with no apparent damage. This was the first time he saw his mother cry. The only other time was at David's wedding in 1964. Jock was buried in a corner of the garden at 1a Clapham Road.

The children all went to the Convent Infant School. Peter and John both went on to Bedford Modern School and did well. John says that they missed the Catholic atmosphere when they went to the Bedford Modern School. However, as it was Wartime, with many of the teachers having been called up they did well in spite of the problems. John was confined to 'a long kind of wheel chair' at some point for six months and Peter used to wheel him along to Bedford Park and they would sit in the fresh air and study.

The Catholic faith was important all the time with family rosary each day and the boys all used to serve Mass at Holy Child and St.Joseph church in Midland Road and Benediction in the Convent Chapel. Mary stayed on at the Convent for all her schooling. She was in the Chemists shop on Bromham Road near the school one day and accidentally stuck her hockey stick through the plate glass display case! Luckily Harrison was insured, so Mary was able to say to the Chemist 'Don't worry! My father is insured.'

Another story told about Mary was when the family invited the Parish Priest, Father Mossey, for a meal. Madeleine asked Father Mossey to say grace. He bowed his head and murmured a grace in Latin.

Mary said, 'Now we'll say it properly!' bent her head and led the family in their usual English prayer. Father Mossey said it taught him a lesson and he often quoted Mary in his later talks when he was invited to say grace or speak. The family used to go for days out with Father Mossey to places like Whipsnade zoo.

Michael, Mary, David Simmonds & Roger Clarke.

Mary, Michael and David were friends with a boy called Roger Clarke who lived opposite and whose father had a small factory attached to his house. Mr Clarke was an engineer and once when the boys went into the factory they were drilling holes in aniseed balls and the boys were allowed to eat the drillings. When they asked questions they were told that they were making necklaces for children in Hospital. After the war they learned that the aniseed balls were actually used as delayed action fuses in limpet mines!

Michael remembers an Italian ice cream man called Arpino who sold his ice creams from a three-wheeled car. Another friend who lived in the first house in Clarenden Street was Colin Fowks. He was a school pal of John's and we are still in touch with him after all the years. The Simmonds family rented their flat from Colin's grandfather, Mr. Grice.

Michael has four particular war memories:

1, A gas practice when we all had to wear our gas masks. We saw a car driving along with white smoke coming out of the exhaust. By the time my mother had got all our gas masks on, the gas had reached us and she had not had time to put her own mask on. Mercifully it was only a practice.

2, We were looking out of a window and saw a 'Buzz Bomb' (a flying bomb) going along with fire coming out of its tail, travelling towards Clapham. I believe it landed on a haystack.

3, At one time during the war there was an anti-aircraft gun positioned beside our house, but it was never fired from there.'

4, I remember lying in bed, listening to the air raid siren and praying 'Please God, don't let them drop bombs on our house!'

Harrison often cycled to the shop on his Raleigh 3-speed roadster of the rather heavy but very robust style of the time. Harrison was friends with the manager of 'Stone's Radio' shop next door. They had sold bicycles before the war. Harrison wanted bikes for Peter and John so the man made up two 'Hercules' bikes from spares and other parts and Peter and John had a lot of fun on them.

Harrison often took them out for a ride on a Sunday afternoon. One of the favourite routes being out to Thurleigh, where the U.S. Air Force based their 'Flying Fortresses' for day light raids on Germany. Harrison also taught Michael to ride a bicycle. Once Harrison got Michael cycling down Clarenden Street towards Clapham Road. Michael was going rather fast and Harrison yelled at him to put the brakes on. Michael did not do it and does not know to this day why he did not put the brakes on. Harrison ran after him and just managed to stop him before he got to the main road.

A later photo of Harrison 'doing the books'

The shop still has a lot of old summary books in which Harrison wrote his weekly income and outgoings and David Simmonds has kindly allowed me to study these and quote from them.

(David is currently managing director of Harrison and Simmonds Ltd.) The books run from 1942 to 1978 with a couple of Wages books that date from 1949 to 1955 and from 1955 to 1964.

On 1 June 1942, Cash in hand was £46 9s 7d, in Bank £1276 2s 0d. During that week the takings were Monday, £41 8s 6d, Tuesday, £36 18s 10d, Wednesday, £49 9s 0d, Thursday, £28 1s 0d (Early closing) Friday, £38 1s 6d and Saturday, £64 16s 7d. How times have changed!

The total amount Harrison took then does not even pay the rent for a week today. In September 1942 the rates paid to Bedfordshire Corporation were £31 16s 0d. The Civic Gas Co. got 10s. Listed as wages Harrison puts initials beside amounts, P 30s (Phyllis?) J 27s 6d, M 20s, H & S drew £10 for expenses, NHS £2. I am not sure who J was but the family say that Harrison had various different staff while they were at school and they do not remember all the names. M was probably Madeleine as Peter says she often helped out while Harrison was doing his Observer Corps shifts.

Among the firms mentioned are Oppenheimer, Townsend, Ronson's, Churchman, Sinclair, Wilson, also the more familiar, Players, Gallaher, Dunhill, Ogden and Gerard. The following month shows more firms from which the shop was buying, including Wills, Godfrey Phillips, Lambert & Butler, Solomon, Singleton & Cole and Sobranie. At the end of December Harrison notes that he gave £7 10s 0d as 'Christmas presents for customers & tradespeople.' In February 1943 'New Gates fitted to Shop front' £10 7s 3d. Dollis cigars, £1 8s 0, and to Gledhill for "Till Rolls" £1 0s 6d. A wages book does not seemed to have survived from the wartime.

Harrison's younger brother, Uncle Chris arrived one day on his motorbike. He was a Major in the Army, home on leave from Egypt. He had a large bird (Goose?) attached to the motorbike and the boys remember it was half roasted with the heat from the engine. Phyllis said he was very good looking and looked very smart in his uniform.

In September 1943 Michael started at Rushmoor School in Shakespeare Road, and was joined two years later by David. Michael soon made friends with another Michael whose father, Pat Mortimer, ran several tobacconist shops in Bromham Road, the Arcade and St. Peter's Street Bedford. The first mention in the books of 'Mortimer's' is in 1943 when Harrison paid Pat Mortimer 6s 3d for 'goods'.

The Bromham road shop had a barber behind at which Peter and John used to have hair cuts. Peter describes *'the memorable feature of these visits to the barber was the large stiff rotary brush he would apply to massage the scalp and whisk away any loose hairs after his cutting and clipping work. This brush, something like the road sweeping machines use, was held like a rolling pin between two handles. It was turned by an overhead drive shaft. It was quite an experience being thoroughly 'brushed up' by that machine.'*

One day Harrison showed Michael and David a little cigar case containing three false cigars. (It was most likely inherited from Uncle Ernie as he was the practical joker.)

Michael took the case to Rushmoor School and at break time offered it to the headmaster Major Richardson. He at first declined and when Michael told him that his father said it was quite all right, the Major went to take one. Michael squeezed the sides of the case and the three cigars disappeared. Michael did not wait to see what was the head master's reaction he just took to his heels and ran. He never heard any more so decided the Major must have seen it as the joke it was meant to be.

During the war younger teachers were called up into the Services, so some retired teachers were re-employed. One was Mr. Coppinger, a Dickensian character if ever there was one. He was quite tall, wore spats over his shoes and he carried an umbrella around with him. He had false teeth with black vulcanite gums which jumped up and down as he spoke.

One day Michael said to Mr. Coppinger, 'I am trying aren't I sir?' 'Yes very!' was the reply. Not long afterwards Mr Coppinger was talking to someone and said to Michael, 'Simmonds ask me that question again.' Michael said, 'I am trying hard aren't I Sir?' Sir retorted, 'Oh! You've spoilt it!'

Harrison & Madeleine playing chess to relax during the War.

John Simmonds (Harrison's second son) joined the staff in the shop when he was thirteen and a half early in 1943. John told me recently of the saying that his Dad used to say at that time. 'Its better to smoke in this world than burn in the next.' John now adds 'It's better to do neither!' John remembers that he would start work at 8am and they would close the shop when 'We had nothing to sell.' He also remembers a lady who worked for a while but 'did not last long as she did not really fit in.'

As Peter put it ' *Some of the skill and tact needed in serving the customers during the war must have been to know who was 'regular' enough for under the counter lines! It was a device intended to satisfy and retain loyal patrons in spite of the shortages, especially cigarettes.'*

John, David, Mary, Michael & Peter
Simmonds about 1945

Player's cigarettes were sent to them once a month in big wooden crates that were held together with metal bands. When you cut the band the sides would fall outwards. The art was to time it so that the packets of cigarettes stayed in a neat cube and did not fall all over the place! They would unpack the crates as soon as possible and hide most of the cigarettes at the back of the shop so as to be able to sell them to regular customers.

Peter remembers that during the war Players were sold in plain blue printed packets instead of the full colour packets that were printed before and after the war. He went to see the film of the 'Battle of Britain' after the war and noticed they were using the coloured packets that were actually plain blue at the time of the battle!

It was about this time that Harrison acquired an old treadle-driven wood lathe and they started to make ashtrays. The lathe was at first installed in the kitchen at 1a Clapham Rd. and the sawdust rising from the work descended on pots and pans and all the surfaces so it was not popular with Madeleine. Soon Harrison ordered a larger and better lathe. This one was installed in the bay window of the front bedroom that was shared by Peter and John. Peter says ' *We were not troubled by the sawdust!'*

They acquired lots of off cuts of wood from Mr. Frank Grey who had a timber yard along St John's Street. The wood was turned into the shapes but as it was not heat resistant they had to have an insert. This was a disc of glass and so they put various pictures under the glass. Thus they built up a line of Bedford souvenirs. Some firms even asked them to make special gift ashtrays for Christmas boxes to their clients.

Bedford Observer Corps War Service 3rd Sept. 1939 to 11th May 1945
FRONT ROW C/Obs Love, C/Obs Munton, C/Obs Bryan, Obs/O Nightingale, Obs/O Neate, Obs/Lieut. Tebbs, Obs/Cder N. Fuller, Obs/Lieut. Evans, Obs/O Srawley, Obs/O Hendry, Obs/O. Percival, C/Obs Thody, C/Obs Craig.
SECOND ROW Obs Rosser, C/Obs Stenner, Obs Mann, L/Obs Wareing, Obs Timmins, Gilliatt, Reddish, Hart, Beer, Rush, Perks.
BACK ROW Obs Plewman, Jessup, Hailstone, Andrews, Craddock, T. Ritson, N. H. Simmonds, Lansberry, Chapman & J. Cox.

Nathaniel Harrison Simmonds is fourth from right on back row. Tommy Ritson has been identified by family members. His name was not on the list supplied from the ROC Museum.

Carter Patterson delivered with a horse-drawn covered van. Their vans were green and the Railway company vans were red. Sometimes the two horse-drawn vans would race up the High Street. Often some one with initiative would run out with a shovel to pick up the horse's droppings. They were good for the roses!

In 1944 the shop had a new washbasin fitted by Gales at £1 12s 8d. Electricity from Bedford Corporation was £5 4s 7d. They paid £1 1s 0d for Defence (Trade sub for RAF Comfort fund.)

The firms include Ardaths, British American Tobacco Co, Melbourne Hart, Van Osiran, & Portland Pipe Co. To National Employers Mutual, War Risk (£2000) £2 10s 0d. On 10 June 'Wings for Victory Week' 10s 6d, and the drains were cleaned out for 5s.

The shop was always closed on Good Friday every year. In August 1944 the wages list reads E 30s, J 10s, M 20s, & C 35s. E may have been Edith Smith a sister of Peggy Canny who worked for the shop later on. J would be John Simmonds and C I am not sure about, but it may a Mrs Cullen that Peter remembers. Mrs Cullen's husband was a glazier who used to cut the circular discs of glass to go into the turned wood ashtrays that Peter made.

New firms included Bryant & May, Edwards Ringer & Bigg, Christopher, Rous Fryer and Orlik. At the end of this year John was getting 12s 6d per week. In December the staff all got Christmas extras, C 10, E £7 10s, J £7 10s, the amount for Railwaymen, postmen, dustmen, customers etc was £20.

Nathaniel Harrison Simmonds with a later car.

In April 1945 John's wages went up to 30s, the rates were £34 9s 8d, and Electricity was £5 4s 11d. In May to Turners (for flags for Victory in Europe Day) £4 13s. In June they paid £40 rent as usual to Covington's plus £41 7s 4d for War damage insurance.

About this time, on a lovely sunny day, one of the customers came into the shop, & Harrison said 'What a lovely day it would be for a drive in a car!' The customer, who Michael thinks was Cecil Allen, said he had a car that been laid up all through the war and he was willing to sell it to Harrison for £75.

Harrison bought the car on the spot without even seeing it. The car was a grey and black 1929 Lanchester with pre-selected gears. It had leather seats and a running board and some original mica windows that were yellowish in colour.

The car had been stored in the garages at the bottom of the Bromham Road railway bridge near the corner of Beverley Crescent. There was a brand new unused battery on the back seat, and some petrol in the tank that had jellied with time. The petrol tank was taken out and given to Madeleine who managed to remove all the jellied petrol. The battery was charged up and the car started at the second attempt.

The first of many trips the family had in that car was to Woburn Sands where they stayed at the Swan Hotel and while they were there 'Victory in Japan' day was announced so it was August 14th 1945.

In January 1946 there is a note in the cash book 'Wreath (Mrs Covington) £3 3s 0d.'

Mrs Covington deserved that wreath. The fact that she had sold Harrison the lease at a fixed rent was to benefit Harrison and Simmonds for many years to come.

The Simmonds family moved to 65 Chaucer Road, Bedford about 1945. This was a large double-fronted house with front and back stairs that had stables and half an acre of land. The garden included a tennis court and a large kitchen garden so Madeleine was in her element as she could grow anything, and she loved her garden.

When the house was up for sale there was also a sale of the contents that included a lovely bracket clock that, according to the auctioneer, did not work. Harrison decided to bid for it and got it at a cheap price. When he looked in the back of the clock he saw the safety catch was on. So he switched it off, wound up the clock and it worked perfectly! It had three different chimes and was a real treasure.

They also had a chiming grandmother clock that had been a wedding present for Harrison and Madeleine and later we inherited that clock and we still have it. Harrison also owned a house in Park Avenue at one time, the only one with two balconies. However he sold it without ever having lived in it as it was requisitioned during the war and no end to the requisitioning was in sight.

All the children had their own place where they could make or invent things and do carpentry or photography. The younger boys used to play shops with empty tobacco tins from the shop. The boys were all very inventive. Young John fitted up a sort of walkie-talkie so that Madeleine could call them all in for meals etc. without leaving the kitchen.

We still have some model aeroplanes and cars made by Peter and John. Later Harrison sold half of his garden to Dr Greenish who built his house and surgery on the plot. At this point the tennis court was converted into a lawn with borders, a rockery and apple trees.

After the War, Harrison was able once more to begin to expand the business. There were lots of new firms that supplied goods to Harrison & Simmonds in the next few years. Aluminium & Allied Products, Searchlight Products, Remington, Elkin, Cottam, Wix, and Parker Pen Co. are first mentioned in the years following the end of the war. In February 1947 there is a short list 'Electric Lamps, £1 9s 0d, glass shades 15s 9d, candles 5s 7d, & oil lamp 9s 11d. They must have had a problem with the lighting or power cuts!

The wages now show J 60s, P 30s, I 55s & M 20s. J would be John, P may still be Phyllis but it may be Peggy Canny, who first came soon after the war, I may be Irene or Rene, and M is probably still Madeleine. Still in

February 1947: Goldings supplies 'New Lock & keys for £1 3s 3d.' John went away to do his National Service from 1947 to 1949. It may be that this was when Peggy Canny joined the shop. Peggy was Harrison's God-daughter so was almost family. John joined the Beds & Herts Regiment and was stationed at the barracks in Kempston on the edge of Bedford some of the time.

John Simmonds in the Army 1947-1949

The summary book shows in April 1947 'For fluorescent lighting and heating in shop to Beds. Electrical Installation' they paid £46 16s 9d. '
In June 1947 'Ministry of National Health £4 6s 8d, National Employers Mutual Insurance £6 19s 9d and Beds Corporation Rates £44 9s 0d.'
The wages now show J (?) £3 8s 6d, I (Irene) £2 17s 7d, P (Peggy) £1 10s 10d. EH (Embo) gets her interest of £5 and NHS £10. Carter Patterson got 3s, Post was 10s 8d and the window cleaner still gets 4s 6d. They paid 9d for a dishcloth and 9d for milk and 15s for Lunches.

(This may have been a celebration to say farewell to Phyllis.)   Phyllis finished at Harrison & Simmonds on June 16th 1947.

In August they paid £5 8s 4d to Grey for window stands, 5s 9d for electric bulbs, and stationary 16s. In March 1948 they paid the usual £40 rent to 'Bursar, Trinity College' who had bought the property after Mrs Covington died. In April the rent for 'Showcase in Lime St' was £146 4s 7d, and to Gammons for 'Blinds for show case £4 13s 6d'.

They also gave a donation to 'The Hospital for Sick Children' of £1 1s, and for 'Coffee and cakes for Staff' 6s 11d. The firms in 1948 included, Parkers, Dunhill, Ogdens, Oppenheimers, Marconies, Mackenzie, Carroll, Samuels and Churchman to whom they paid £104 10s 8d. In December a new rubber doormat from Gammons cost £6 16s 9d, and the Christmas presents totalled £20.

Arthur Finding with N. H. Simmonds in the shop

Harrison & Simmonds also took on another man called Arthur Finding. Arthur worked in the shop from about 1947 until 1960. He became a great friend to Harrison and after he retired he still came back to help with the Christmas rush. Arthur came to them from the firm of Mortimer's.

Pat Mortimer and his son Michael also had a shop on Bromham Road and the two families were friends as well as fellow tobacconists. The friends would often direct a customer round to the other shop, if they could not supply the customer's needs. Michael Mortimer told me that Harrison said to him once 'If you have not dusted a tin of tobacco, just pick it up and wipe it on your trousers as you bring it to the counter. Then no-one will know you have not dusted!'

Michael Mortimer and Michael Simmonds had been at school together at Rushmoor Preparatory School when boys and have been close friends ever since. Michael Simmonds is Godfather to Michael Mortimer's son Kevin and Michael Mortimer is Godfather to our daughter Bernadette.

Michael Mortimer is also a member of the Secular Franciscan Order so he is a spiritual brother to Michael & me.

During that same year 1948 Harrison and Madeleine decided to send Michael and David to a Catholic boarding school. Michael started at Ratcliffe College, near Leicester in the summer term of 1948 and David started at Grace Dieu Manor that was the preparatory school for Ratcliffe College that same year.

David & Michael Simmonds about the time they went to Ratcliffe College

They both did well at school and benefited from the Catholic atmosphere of the school. Michael also says that Ratcliffe was the 'saving of him' as he had been a great trial to his parents before he went there, but Ratcliffe helped him to know what was right and wrong.

Harrison said once that he could not have afforded to send the boys to boarding school before that time or afterwards but he felt that the Good Lord had given him the money just when he needed it for the boys education. The weekly takings of Harrison & Simmonds in 1949 were now into four figures as the value of money decreased.

Edith Fanny came and lived with the family, after she retired from Wellington College, in 1948, when she was almost eighty years old! Michael remembers her birthday party and how Madeleine made a special birthday cake and carried it into the room with all eighty candles blazing so that all the flames merged into one large flame.

Soon after this, one morning Madeleine knocked and went into her mother-in-law's room and found Edith Fanny unconscious, lying on the floor in front of the gas fire, which was switched on but not lit! Madeleine quickly turned off the gas, opened the windows and sent for the Doctor.

Edith Fanny had bent down to put on the gas and then in getting up to find the matches had banged her head on the cast iron mantleshelf, and knocked herself out. Edith Fanny soon recovered.

Fancy Dress Party at Chaucer Road, Back: Michael as Charlie Chaplin, Buster & Kit Brown, Ernie Swain. Seated Mary as Dick Whittington with David as the cat, Madeleine, Aunt Embo and Nora O'Neil. About 1950.

Uncle Chris. Simmonds (Harrison's brother) had married a nurse, Elizabeth Hesketh, whom he met while serving in Egypt. They married and had their first child Christopher David, born 1948, in Egypt. When their son was still a baby they returned to England and stayed at first with Harrison and Madeleine in Chaucer Road.

Then they got a house at Bromham and lived there for a while before moving down to Abbots Road in Abingdon not far from Oxford. They had three daughters; Sally in 1950, Jane in 1952 and Vanessa in 1958. Sally remembers visiting '*Uncle Nat's shop*' and '*He used to give my father a new pipe every time we visited!*' Also '*Uncle Nat used to keep a piece of raw potato in the tobacco jars to keep the tobacco moist.*'

After the relations moved out Madeleine and Harrison had several different lodgers. Among them was a photographer, Ernie Swain who became a great friend and Nora O'Neil, who had the room that had formerly been Edith Fanny's. Madeleine used to visit people in hospital and that is how she met Nora. There had been a fire in Nora's home and her mother had died so she was alone and her home not fit to live in so she came and lived with the Simmonds for some years.

Michael remembers being involved at school with Oscar Wilde's play 'The Importance of Being Ernest' and he was always quoting from Oscar Wilde so at Christmas 1951 Nora gave him a book 'The collected works of Oscar Wilde' which he still has.

After the war Harrison called his tobacco blends after Dickens characters, as he was very fond of Dickens books. We have a leaflet that advertised and described some of these blends. I am told it was about 1960. It is headed

The Dickens range of Speciality Tobaccos.

We at Harrison and Simmonds since we were established have specialised in offering a wide variety of pipe tobaccos, which now include the traditional style of blends and flakes of enduring repute as well as the more adventurous richer mixtures and the milder aromatics of more recent years. Unlike the mass produced tobacco's, most of the range are blended by hand and offer a unique assortment from which the discerning pipe man may find his individual requirement.

Captain Cuttle (Triple flake) A master blend of three flakes, slow burning cool and satisfying, a secret recipe blended on the premises for several decades- the perfect balance- when found make a note of.

Scrooge (Turkish mixture) A unique mixture of a secret recipe of Virginia and Latakia tobaccos with a generous proportion of Turkish- blended on the premises for many years- rich distinctive and recognizable aroma- broad cut, medium strength.

Micawber A very palatable mild slightly sweetened broken flake of an excellent texture with a touch of rum and maple to stimulate the brain and uplift the heart.

David Copperfield Broad cut mixture of long time fermented dark Virginia leaf and toasted Burley- good nose, cool and fragrant- a gentle smoke.

Peggotty Fully ripe Virginia and Burley tobacco rounded with a full caramel aroma soft and very mild, ideal for the beginner.

Barnaby Rudge A fragrant, short cut Virginia with a fruity plum flavoured aroma, suitable for the novice

Pickwick A fruity tobacco with an apple aroma base and some liquorice - rubbed out mild and slow burning

Sam Weller A fine cut ready rubbed Virginia with a distinctive nose, modestly priced, medium strength- a quiet and agreeable flavour.

Oliver Twist Traditional black pigtail twist - strong and cool. A well-known tobacco of yesteryear which has survived generations.

Fagin "A man's tobacco" good wholesome dark flake of great satisfaction with its own distinctive flavour- not for the novice.

The Dodger A quality smoke with a high proportion of black Cavendish with a good bright Virginia- full bodied with maple aroma- chunky cut.'

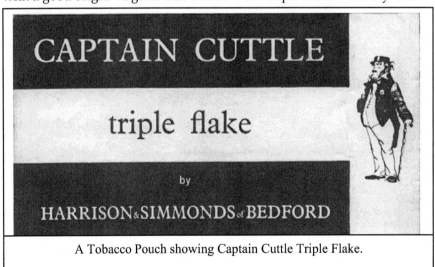

A Tobacco Pouch showing Captain Cuttle Triple Flake.

Apparently Harrison said once about 'Scrooge,' 'My tobacco blends are the poor mans Balkan Sobranie.' Balkan Sobranie was one of the more expensive tobaccos. To this day some of Harrison's mixtures are still sold in the shop. John remembered a big tall man who used to smoke a very big pipe. John remembers his Dad joking with this man who was a good customer for one of Harrison's blends.

Harrison's sister Edith Mousley was widowed in 1950 and she decided to come and live in Bedford and her mother Edith Fanny went to live with her at 87 Goldington Road, Bedford, now they were both widows. Edith's daughter Pat Mousley, was now at Reed's School, the same school that Harrison and Edith had attended but under a different name. Edith began to 'do the books' at the shop. She also still made powder puffs with the machine that her husband had left her that was now in the stables at the back of the shop.

Peter Simmonds en route to Rome
1950

Apparently Edith also used to do engravings on pens in those early days as Pat remembers that she and her Grandma (Edith Fanny), both had pens with their names engraved on them by her Mum.

Harrison's eldest son Peter had been apprenticed for four years at De Havillands at Hatfield, on 20 November 1944, learning to design aircraft. He left them about 1950 and spent time making ashtrays for the shop and studying.

This may be when Pat Mousley (Ede's daughter) remembered painting the coats of arms of the Bedford schools. Peter says they had transfers so the transfers may have been made from Pat's paintings.

When Michael and I visited the Town Hall some years ago we were quite amused to see that some of Peter's 'Harrison & Simmonds' ashtrays were still put out for use. Our daughter Maria still has one she uses as a photo frame.

Also during 1950 as it was a 'Holy Year' Peter decided to cycle to Rome on pilgrimage with a friend. They left on August 5th and arrived in Rome on 21st August. They cycled across France staying in Rouen, Paris Dijon, then over the Jura Alps to Lake Geneva. Then through St. Bernard's pass into Italy. They visited Aosta, Turin, Florence and Bologna on the way to Rome.

They spent several days in Rome visiting all the main churches etc. and they were present at a big audience with the Pope Pius XII. Then on the way home they cycled up the east coast of Italy, past Genoa where they were very shaken by the cobblestones, and along the Italian Riviera and on to Monte Carlo. Peter and his friend cycled up through Marseilles, Orleans and Chartres to Dieppe.

They arrived back in England on September 6th very tired but exhilarated with their achievement. Then in 1952 Peter entered the Salesians of Don Bosco Order as a Lay Brother. He was sent out to Cape Town the following year and has worked there ever since. Peter has lived and worked most of the time in the Salesian Institute.

The Salesians take boys off the street and teach them a trade as well as giving them a home. Peter has been a teacher of woodwork and cabinet making, headmaster of the school and has also worked running the repository that sells religious articles and books to the whole of South Africa. He also lived and worked for some years at the parish of Lansdowne on the edge of Cape Town.

Among the Simmonds friends were the family of Dr. Leahy; he had three sons and a daughter Elizabeth. They lived on the corner of Bromham Road and Union Street and they often met at church so the two families became friends. Anthony Leahy and Mary Simmonds were both interested in farming and used to go round in a group with several other young people. They often borrowed the Doctor's car on a Sunday after Mass and Elizabeth says her father would be worried for fear the car did not return intact for his round on Monday!

On November 3rd 1951 Harrison & Madeleine celebrated their silver wedding anniversary. Among the guests were Harrisons' sisters Edith, Ellen & Mary, Aunt Embo, Edith Fanny, Buster & Kit Brown, Elizabeth and Anthony Leahy and several other friends. Ernie Swain took the photographs.

Nathaniel Harrison and Madeleine Simmonds cutting their Silver Wedding cake, November 3rd 1951. Photo by Ernie Swain.

It was in 1952 Coronation year, that Harrison & Simmonds took part in an exhibition in the Corn Exchange and they won second prize for their display.

Harrison & Simmonds' Winning display 1952

John Simmonds had done his National service from 1947-1949. He came back to the shop to work but then in the early 1950's he felt called to follow St Francis, so he entered the Order of Friars Minor as a Lay Brother.

He left the shop at Christmas 1953, his last wage of £7 10s was paid on 26th December and he entered the Order in January 1954. He was known in the Order as Brother Simon OFM. After his noviciate he spent some time at East Bergholt in Suffolk, then at Chilworth near Guildford. John was later sent up to work in Osmotherly in Yorkshire where he worked for about twenty years, housekeeping, teaching and nursing.

Although Harrison was happy for John to become a Franciscan, it meant he left the shop and Harrison felt he could not go on alone in the shop without family support, so he decided to sell the business! Harrison actually contacted the Imperial Tobacco Company and invited them to come to inspect the shop. Harrison thought they might keep him on as manager. He wrote to Michael at school and told him what he planned. Michael was horrified and wrote back and said he would like to come and work in the shop.

Nathaniel Harrison Simmonds c.1960

So Michael left school on 10 December 1953 and came home to work in the shop. Michael clearly remembers the day the representatives came from the Imperial Tobacco Company to the house at Chaucer Road.

They arrived in a Rolls Royce car and stopped just up the road. Harrison went up to them and told them that circumstances had changed and the sale was off.

Michael says the first time he served a customer it was like walking the plank! However he soon began to find it fun and he is very good salesman and always willing to put himself out to please a customer. Michael met a girl who was the daughter of a customer and he asked her out. They went to the cinema to see the Glenn Miller Story. Then he invited her home to meet his parents. Only then did he ask her age and she was only 13! So he stopped asking her out and later she married an American and went to live in the USA.

In 1954 Michael went to Ronsons to do a two-day course in repairs of their lighters. Soon afterwards a man from Colibri came and instructed Michael about the Colibri Lighters.

So Harrison and Simmonds became agents for repairs of both Ronsons and Colibri Lighters. There was a gas jet fitted in the shop so that they could light the customer's cigars and cigarettes. After a few years they began to feel this was a bit old fashioned so Michael suggested that they adapt a Variflame lighter and so with the permission of Ronsons and the aid of the gas company the gas flame now came out of the lighter.

On 11 January 1951 a new family came to Bedford who were to be very close friends with the Simmonds family. Jack Davies was the new manager at Hockcliffe's the stationary shop up the High Street on the corner of Lime Street. Jack and his wife Una and their two sons Harold and Hugh soon became close to the family as well as Jack being a business colleague.

Every morning at about 10-30 a group of business friends would meet up at the Cadena Cafe on the corner of the Arcade. They included Johnny Cox (manager of Cadena), Tommy Ritson, an insurance agent, Jack Davies from Hockcliffe's, Butch Cleaver the manager of Frames Travel agent, Cecil Allan (who lived in Park Avenue and was also in insurance) Buster Brown manager at Sketchley's Cleaners and his wife Kit, Reg. Bustin (Phyllis's husband who was an accountant) and Nathaniel H. Simmonds. They all had morning tea or coffee and exchanged news and information about the business world. They were all very good friends as well as being business colleagues.

Michael Simmonds in the Army

Michael went away to do his National service for two years on 3 February 1955, after just over a year in the shop. Michael was a signaller in the Army and learned Morse code etc. That same week David Simmonds started work in the shop.

During that same year 1955 the Simmonds family moved out to 'The Moorings' 112 Bromham Road, Biddenham, it was just up the road from Bromham Bridge. Here they owned a smallholding beside the river Great Ouse.

There in the paddock Mary kept cows and Madeleine had 100 chickens in deep litter. They also had two dogs and a cat. Mary Simmonds had a very special relationship with her cows. Once when she had been away on holiday, she arrived home and went straight to the gate into the field. Then she called 'Fairy' and her favourite cow came galloping up the field to greet her!

N. Harrison Simmonds with his daughter Mary at the Moorings

There still exists part of a diary that Edith Fanny Simmonds used to write in at odd times. On March 11th 1955 she wrote: -
'Harrison and Mary came and told us about the new calf'"
3rd. April " Michael and David came am, Madeleine and Harrison pm. Letter from Bert, Alice is rambling!
13th April, Alice not so well. Nellie and Mary and Elsie came to tea from Newport Pagnell'
Edith Fanny's daughter Ellen, 'Aunt Nell,' was nursing in Newport Pagnell and her sister Mary with Mary's friend Elsie must have been staying with her. Mary and Elsie shared a house for many years.
'24th April Harrison & Madeleine and Michael came, Michael is returning to camp. Harrison went to see Pat back to school and then to Worthing to stay with Buster & Kit Brown.

July 21st. Ede to Pats school prize day.
Nov 23rd. "Family gathering for birthday, 17 cards and some useful presents.
Harrison & Madeleine, Chris, and Mary Simmonds came'

When Michael came out of the Army early in 1957, he worked on the smallholding for a while with Mary and Madeleine. Then Jack Davies got Michael a job over in Aylesbury at their branch of W.H. Smith. Michael used to go over to Aylesbury by moped. He had fixed a small 'PowerPak' engine on to his pushbike and thus was able to travel home at the weekends.

Later he bought an L. E. Velocette motorbike. Michael worked in Aylesbury from March until Christmas 1957. During that time he often used to go to Abingdon to visit Uncle Chris and his family who were now living there. Aunt Elizabeth (known as Aunt Fizz) used to be worried by him going all that way on the motorbike. Then in January 1958 he went to a Salesian house at Bollington near Macclesfield to try his vocation as a Salesian brother.

Harrison & Madeleine with their PowerPak bicycles

Harrison and his wife also had 'Power Pak's motors on their bicycles. Harrison was on his way home to the Moorings one evening after work. He was cycling along Bromham Road near the Moorings, put his arm out to show he was turning right and began to pull out.

Suddenly a car came from behind to overtake him. Harrison was caught and dragged along the road a short way until the car stopped. The driver turned out to be the insurance agent who was Tommy Ritson's boss! The gentleman was very apologetic. Harrison picked himself and the bike up and was only slightly grazed.

He went into the house shouting 'I'm alive, I'm alive.'

In June of 1958 David was called up for his National Service, he became an officer and spent much of the two years stationed in Edinburgh castle. This again left Harrison alone apart from employees.

Michael had been having doubts about his work in the Salesians, so when he heard from his father that he was alone again, Michael went to see Father O'Brian (his Salesian superior) and told him he felt he was needed at home and in the shop again. So Michael returned in September 1958 and after David returned from his National Service in 1960, Harrison made them both partners with him in Harrison & Simmonds.

Charlie Emmerson was working with Harrison at that time and he stayed for about ten years. The shop employed an elderly lady called Mrs Robinson who used to clean the shop for them. Mrs Robinson was very deaf but very willing. She used to look up when scrubbing the floor and say "Oh! I love work!" At that time the toilet was still down the yard, with a padlock on the door. One day Harrison was in the toilet and Mrs Robinson saw the padlock was not fastened and promptly did it up, and departed.

Harrison shouted and shouted and eventually someone from Stone's Radio shop next door heard him and told the people in the shop and he was released. The floor in the toilet was very uneven so you had to give a great shove at the door to get in. Michael decided to do something about it, so he spent time taking up the tiles and relaying them so that the door did not stick. He told everyone in the shop but forgot Mrs Robinson. The next time she went to clean the toilet she gave the usual hard shove at the door and nearly did a header into the toilet basin!

Jack & Una Davies and their sons Hugh and Harold became very close to the Simmonds Family. Una Davies told me that Madeleine was the kindest, most thoughtful person she has ever known. Madeleine would arrive at Una's house in Cowper Road, for coffee, with a large bunch of beautifully arranged flowers fresh from her garden and say to Una 'Its the anniversary of Harold going to University,' or 'Its your wedding anniversary' or some other special day, often something Una had totally forgotten!

The Simmonds Family sprung a surprise on Jack Davies when he had a big birthday. It was 13 August 1959. They had invited the Davies family for tea on a Sunday afternoon. Jack was working in his garden and was quite reluctant to leave it to go out to tea. Una persuaded him to leave the garden and change.

When they approached the Moorings they saw lots of balloons and Jack said to Una 'Oh they've got something special on, maybe we had better not go!' However Una said 'They are expecting us!' and she persuaded him so they arrived and were greeted with a 'This is your Life' party.

Michael was the 'Eamon Andrews' and they told Jack all about his life amid great hilarity! Lots of their other friends were there and the photographs, which Una still treasures, were taken by Ernie Swain. All except the one shown below, which was taken by Michael Simmonds, on Ernie Swain's camera. It was a good day for Una and Jack.

The 'This is your Life' Party. Back row: Butch Cleaver, Tommy Ritson, Una Davies, Harrison, Madeleine, Jack Davies, Reg Bustin, Ernie Swain & Cecil Allen. Front row: Mrs Cleaver, Harold Davies, Miss Cleaver, Hugh Davies, Mrs Ritson, Phyllis Bustin & Mrs Allen.

At this time I was puzzled by the rent entries in the books as they were paid to 'Stone's Radio Co' and I understood that Trinity College in Cambridge were the landlords. However it was explained that as Harrison & Simmonds were only 78a, thus the smaller half of the building, the rent was paid to the larger shop and then Stone's paid the rent for the whole property to Trinity College.

The shop had different plastic tobacco pouches printed with the name of the supplier. We still have some of the old pouches that can no longer be used, as since 1971 they have to have a 'Health warning' on them. I have some of them here as I write, 'Forrestal importers of fine American pipe tobacco'. 'Charles Fairmorn (UK) Ltd, sole UK importers of Macbaren-Von Eicken, and Peter Stokkeybye Tobacco's.' 'Gawith & Hoggarth's loose tobaccos.' 'Kendal exclusive Radfords.' (Sic) and another from Gawith & Hoggarth's without the extra writing on it, just the pipe picture.

Mary Simmonds & Ernest Shiner leave the church after their wedding.
4 March 1957. Pat Mousley is the bridesmaid in the background

There is a story told about Tommy Ritson coming into the shop and saying to Harrison 'I bet I can make you get up your ladder.' Harrison said 'I bet you can't.' Tommy was about to light a cigarette but instead of putting the flame to his cigarette he threw the lighted match up onto the shelf full of boxes of Swan matches! Harrison got the ladder out fast and was up it in record time! This from Tommy Ritson who was the insurance agent! Tommy won his bet!

Harrison decided to buy an embossing machine for producing colour price tickets for his window displays. He asked his dear friend Johnny Cox (manager of the Cadena Café in the Arcade) to come with his hand trolley and help him fetch the machine. The two were pushing the trolley back down Lime St. when Harrison saw one of his posh lady customers approaching, so he left Johnny to push the trolley and went ahead saying to the lady 'Good Afternoon Madam!' then when she had gone he went back to help Johnny Cox. They were both laughing!

Mary Simmonds was married on 4th March 1957 to Ernest Shiner, a farmer. The wedding was at Holy Child & St.Joseph Church in Midland

Road and the reception was held at Aunt Ede's home at 87 Goldington Road where there were big rooms.

Mary and Ernie lived at first in a caravan at 'The Moorings' until Ernest had built them a house at Lower East End Farm, near Cranfield and they moved out there to live. Mary had her first two sons Nicholas and Francis while living in the caravan.

They even got a second small caravan that was linked as an extra room for the boys to sleep in. Mary and Ernie had another three sons Richard, Bernard and Stephen, after moving out to the farm at Cranfield and finally a daughter Theresa who was born the same year as our Clare 1967.

All their children are now married with families of their own. Nicholas has two sons and two daughters. Francis has two sons. Richard and his wife Joanne now live at the farm where he was born and they have three sons, including Thomas who is now one of the staff at Harrison & Simmonds. Stephen and Bernard have three daughters each, and Theresa and her husband have three sons.

Mary died from breast cancer on 17th February 1986. Ernie died on 11th July 2000. Peter was at home when Mary died and was here for Ernie's funeral also. He has always been a great comfort at these times.

In 1961 the Harrison Bible was found in the Wheatsheaf Inn in Salisbury and it came eventually to the hands of Edith Fanny Simmonds, Harrison's mother, who was now living in Bedford with her daughter Edith Mousley who was also a widow.

On Sunday 30 July 1961 there was a family gathering in the garden at the Moorings. Michael made a tape recording saying 'Good afternoon Mrs. Simmonds,' his Grandma replied 'Good Evening Sir!' So he asked her to say something into the tape recorder. Edith Fanny said 'Now what shall I say, and what shall I do and what shall I sing!'

Michael said 'Anything you like Madam!'

The last photo taken of Edith Fanny Simmonds

So Edith Fanny started to sing in her cracked old voice.

'Tell me one thing; tell me truly, tell me why you scorn me so.

Tell me why, when men ask a question, you should always answer No!, No Sir, No Sir, No Sir, No!

If I were walking in the garden, I should ask you to be mine. No Sir, No Sir, No Sir, No!'

She went on singing for several more verses and every time Michael said 'Thank you' she did not hear him and just carried on singing. The tape has picked up the laughing of the rest of the party.

Next Michael turned to Aunt Embo and said 'Good Evening Mrs Harrison' and asked after her health. Aunt Embo replied that she 'was much better' and then told a tale about Uncle Dick. 'He went to London on a stick, the stick broke and sent him off to Basingstoke!' Michael had been playing a recording of John (Bro. Simon) and he asked Embo about it and she said it was 'Very enjoyable.' Michael said he could not get Pat to say anything.

However he did get Ede to speak and she said laughingly that 'I thought my mother was never going to stop!' Michael went next to his father and Harrison launched into the story of a gentleman who was a little over weight.

'So he went to see the doctor who gave him some pills to lose weight. He should lose 2 lbs each day. He took the pill and went to bed. He had beautiful dreams about being chased by a lot of beautiful blondes! In the morning he had lost 2 lbs. So he took the pills again and the dream was repeated and he lost the weight. After a week he had lost 14 lbs and was very pleased so he stopped taking the pills. Soon afterwards he was speaking to friend of his who also suffered with over weight, so he advised him to see the doctor and ask for the same pills. The friend did as he had been advised and got the pills from his doctor, but when he took the pill and went to sleep, his dreams were of being chased by lions and tigers and it was awful, but in the morning he had lost the 2 lbs so he thought he had better go on taking the pills. At the end of the week he had lost 14 lbs and was very glad to stop taking the pills. So he went back to the doctor and asked him how it was that his friend had had such beautiful dreams and he had such awful dreams. The doctor said "Oh that's easy, your friend is a private patient, and you are on the National Health!" '

There was great hilarity after that and Michael told Edith Fanny, who was very deaf, that he would turn it up loud for her so she could hear the joke. Later she started to sing 'Where are you going to my pretty maid.' But she said she could not sing.

Both Harrison and Michael tried to get her to tell them about her courting days. She came out with a tale about a man asking a chemist for a love potion and his girl telling him that two cabbages that look alike are ditto! Then she got in a muddle and everyone laughed at her. Next Embo told the story about Ernie putting his foot in Louie's lap. Michael said 'He really put his foot in it!'

They told stories about Auntie Cathy Harrison always being the boss of the family and if anyone found something useful on their walks home from school she always said she had dropped it on her way.

Harrison congratulated Pat on passing her examinations so successfully. Ede said that Grandma was still making things even aged over ninety. This tape gives a sound picture of a typical Simmonds family gathering, with jokes and banter and affection all round.

Only a few weeks later Aunt Embo died on 2nd September 1961. She was cremated and her ashes buried with her husband's at Elstow Abbey. Their tombstone reads:- "IN LOVING MEMORY OF ERNEST THE BELOVED HUSBAND OF EMILY ADELAIDE HARRISON, WHO FELL ASLEEP 13TH. APRIL 1938, AGED 66 YEARS. UNTIL WE MEET AGAIN. AND EMILY ADELAIDE HIS WIFE WHO DIED 2 SEPTEMBER 1961 AGED 83 YEARS. REUNITED."

Edith Fanny was stone deaf and had been for many years. When she was dying she said to Ede 'Have you got the wireless on? What's that beautiful music I hear!' Edith Fanny died on 8 January 1962. She had been a widow for fifty-five years.

From the Beds Times. Jan 1962

'The recent death at the age of 93 of Mrs Edith Fanny Simmonds of 87 Goldington Road, calls to mind the large families of Victorian days. Mrs Simmonds, mother of the High Street Tobacconist Mr. Nathaniel Harrison Simmonds, was one of the fourteen children of Mr. J. P. Harrison and his wife of Salisbury. She was also one of three sets of twins to which the Victorian Mrs Harrison was addicted, and was the last survivor of the Harrison family of that generation. Some time ago the Harrison Family Bible was discovered by workmen, modernising the Wheatsheaf Inn, Salisbury. The Bible recorded the births of the fourteen children between March 1862 and February 1875. The father of this formidable family was a qualified Chemist'

From another cutting

'The last surviving member of an old Salisbury family, Mrs Edith Fanny Simmonds, of 87 Goldington Road, Bedford died on Sunday aged 93. Mrs Simmonds, who was the mother of Mr N. H. Simmonds of Harrison and Simmonds High Street, Bedford had lived with her widowed daughter for ten years. She had been a widow for fifty five years and is survived by two sons and three daughters. The funeral service today (Friday) at Elstow Parish Church at noon will be conducted by the Rev. P. J. Hartley.'

She was buried in Elstow Abbey Churchyard near to her brother Ernest & Embo. Her tombstone has the inscription:- 'IN LOVING MEMORY OF OUR DEAR MOTHER EDITH FANNY SIMMONDS WHO DIED ON 9TH JAN. 1962 AGED 93 YEARS, AND OF MARY HER DAUGHTER WHO DIED ON 4TH JULY 1965, AGED 61 YEARS.'

Michael was ill in bed with pneumonia when his Grandma died. He had been at choir practice at Church when he began to feel ill. So he came home and put himself to bed. When he woke up he tried to get up and could not move so he called feebly for his mother. She did not believe at first that he was so weak but she sent for the doctor and he diagnosed pneumonia! So Michael was off from the shop for three weeks.

Soon after this Michael won £50-0 on a premium bond. By chance Peter was home on leave from Cape Town so he decided to take Peter to Lourdes on a brief pilgrimage. Harrison insisted on paying for Peter so Michael only had to pay for himself. They had a happy and prayerful visit to the French shrine.

David Simmonds & Liliane Pace on their wedding day 10th September 1964.

In 1963 I first saw the shop as I described earlier. Michael and David & Peggy were the staff with Harrison and all seemed to be going smoothly.

Michael remembered Peggy Canny saying sadly one day 'No one ever calls me by my name!' From that time on Michael always called her Margaret, although she was still Peggy to everyone else.

In 1964 Harrison was ill early in the year and both Michael and David were married. Among the wedding presents were two four-inch high beautifully curved pewter jugs with a letter:-

From the House of Orlik,
17-18 Old Bond Street,
London W 1.
Whereas it has come to the notice of the House of Orlik and its satellite Company Tallent & Bennett, that the junior offspring of the venerable house of Harrison & Simmonds , County Tobacconists have nuptial ceremonies impending.

Kindly take notice that the said Houses deem it seemly to bestow on the offspring namely Michael Simmonds and David Simmonds a small token of their esteem.

Pat Mortimer and Michael Simmonds ready for the Charter year Pageant

We therefore give notice of the dispatch under separate cover two pewter jugs of a suitable size to contain a few drops of oil, to be used very occasionally on turbulent waters, a not unheard- of expediency in the happiest of marriages.

Signed 27th day of July 1964 for and on behalf of the House of Orlik.
R. W. Smith.

Our tiny pewter jug still has pride of place on our front room mantle piece although it is slightly battered from the children playing with it!

Another special deal that Harrison did, was with Barlings Pipes, He bought the 'Barlings Londoner' pipe by the gross at a reduced price. They also sold special 'Charter Pipes' in Charter year 1966.

During the Charter year pageant Michael Simmonds played Mace Bearer to Pat Mortimer's Mayor. They looked quite comical as Pat Mortimer was short and stout and

Michael is tall and thin and processing along in 18th century costume with tricorne hats and fur trimmed robes they were quite a sight.

Harrison & Simmonds were successful in a Charter year window dressing competition in 1966. The certificate reads:- *'This is to record that Harrison & Simmonds were awarded Second Prize in the Window Dressing Competition organised by Bedford Chamber of Trade as part of the Celebrations commemorating the 800th. Anniversary of the granting of the Charter by King Henry II in 1166.* Dated this 9th. Day of May 1966.
Ronald Whittingham. MAYOR

Early in 1967 Harrison and Madeleine, with Alice Cullen (Madeleine's God mother) had a six week cruise holiday to Cape Town to visit Bro. Peter. We still have some of the slides that they took and a brief diary that was kept of the voyage.

'Friday 27th January. Depart. Rough and noisy during the night. Alice in Bed on Saturday 28th. Sun came out after lunch. Passing out of Bay of Biscay 6-30pm Very windy out of doors but had a short walk. Captain's Cocktail party in evening.

Harrison & Madeleine meeting the Captain

Sunday 29th Mass at 10-00 am. Warm and sunny on Deck. Illustrated talk by Captain on the Bridge and the ship.

Monday 30th. Landed at Las Palmas. Volcanic mountains, beautiful scenery, plenty of colourful flowers, wild geraniums, hibiscus, bougainvillea, poinsettias, 6 ft. high or more. Banana plantations, vines tomatoes and potatoes. Spanish dancers came on board. We had a country coach tour. Film in evening.

Tuesday had hairdo. Very hot with slight breeze. Raining in evening.

Wed. Feb. 1st Children's sports and Vaal Derby with Ascot Hats.

Thursday Very chill & heavy. Children's party and fancy dress.

Friday. Crossed the Equator 6-30 am. Ceremony of crossing the Line. Tour of the Galley. There was a Gala dance for those who wanted it followed by bacon and egg breakfast at Midnight in the Galley.

Saturday. Played Bingo won 30/- for 5/- Films of South Africa. Flying fish abundant.

Sunday February 5th. Mass 10-00 am. Transparencies shown in cinema of film taken during the trip.

Monday Feb.6th. Very lazy day fine but rather windy. Played bingo. Filled in customs forms

Wednesday 8th. Went on deck to see sunrise over Table Mountain 6-15 am. Went to Mass & then into Immigration. While waiting in queue Peter came up and found us. Came on board with a boarding ticket. Went though customs & then down to breakfast. Landed 9 am. Had long wait for luggage in Customs shed. Alice's friend Pat met us with car & brought us all to Hotel. Flowers in bedrooms from Pat. Went for a drive in Pats car till lunch time. Lunch in Botanical gardens with pigeons for company. Tea at Sea Point & S.A. Museum. Dinner and early bed. Also visited Anglican Cathedral.

Thursday 9th. Went to Kirstenbosch Gardens. Very beautiful. Good lunch in restaurant. Went over the (Salesian) Institute and had tea there. Peter stayed for dinner at Hotel. Went for a walk after dinner, early bed.

Friday 10th. Went up tallest building and had a drink. Too windy for roof. Went over Cape Town Castle. Very interesting. Lunch at the Institute, spent afternoon making tape and then had tea. Peter had dinner with us and then had very nice walk round Seapoint.

Saturday 11th. Table Mountain and lunch at the top. Drive with Father Calussi in the afternoon. Went to Pats for dinner. Collected and brought back by her parents. Posted Tape. (We still have it!)

Sunday 12th. Mass at 10-30 am. Cliff took us out all round coast to Cape point. Had lunch in the woods; food provided by the Institute and Cliff. Went for miles through nature reserve but only saw zebras and buck. Had tea at Cape Point , but *did not climb to top. Home via Chapman's peak, Simonstown, FishHoek, Haut Bay, & Camps bay. On the way out in the morning visited Rhodes memorial & Zoo. Peter stayed for dinner. Visited Church nearby.*

Madeleine and Bro. Peter Simmonds with Alice Cullen at Sea Point, Cape Town.

<u>Monday 13-2-67</u> *Dutch Reformed Church. R.C.Cathedral, City Hall, Koofmens de Wet House, Cultural History Museum. Shopping for gifts in Curio shop. Walk to Seapoint after dinner.*
<u>Tuesday 14th. Feb.</u> *Wrote Postcards. Collected car from Mini car hire at 12 o'clock, after walk and drink at botanical gardens. Went to Hout Bay for lunch. (rather expensive) Beautiful Crayfish. Then drove to Landsdowne, had tea and were shown round school and grounds.*

Back to Hotel for dinner with Peter and then up to Signal hill to view the lights of Cape Town.
<u>Wednesday 15th.</u> *Bought picnic lunch & went Table Mountain Road to eat it. Visited Mrs Morris. Went to Llandudno, collected shells & M had a paddle. Open Air "Macbeth" after dinner.*
<u>Thursday 16th.</u> *Drive with Pat, morning tea with Mrs ?Lower?, lunch at Institute, drove to Bird sanctuary, flamingos, herons, pelicans etc. Then drove home via Chapmans peak. After dinner visited Mr Pagano.*

Friday 17ᵗʰ Bought Trousers & shoes & picnic lunch. Went to Steenbros Dam and reservoir, then Gordon's Bay and strand. Walked along the front at Camp Bay after dinner and had a sprinkling of rain on our way home.

Saturday 18ᵗʰ. Shopping in Town then lunch at Harbour Restaurant. Went to Silvermyn Reserve woods up in the mountains. Walk after dinner along Sea Point Front.

Sunday 19ᵗʰ. Mass at 10-30 am. Then out to Sir Sowry's pass gardens. Had picnic lunch in the woods then through the winding road through the mountains to Fransch Hock and Hellshoogte and came across overturned car on loose gravelled bend.

Monday 20ᵗʰ. Depart 9-30 for Paarl interesting visit to KWV (Kooperative Winehouses Vereenigins) cellars etc. Tasted samples of various vines.

After lunch toured Rembrant Cigarette factory where are made 25,000,000 per day. Called at Catholic Church and then to Wellington before returning to Cape Town.

Tuesday. Visited Institute to buy a few things, then to Sea Point. Visited Aquarium and then took car back to owners. 613 miles in one week.

Lunch at Hildebrande's & then shopping. Back to Hotel to do packing and then supper with Pat.

Wednesday 22ⁿᵈ. Pat fetched us at 10-30 to take luggage to Docks. Dealt with passports and then had luggage taken on board. Locked up our cabins and went for lunch in Town with Pat and Peter. Returned to boat to let Pat see over the ship. She left at 2 o'clock to fetch Susan from school. Peter stayed on board until 3-30 then watched us from the dock. Joined by Pat and Susan about 3-50. Hundreds of streamers thrown from the ship to the crowds below. Very pretty sight. Photographers took pictures of passengers. Whistle blew at 4 o'clock & boat started to move. Very soon right out in the bay and Peter out of sight. Went for a cup of tea and then unpacked. Early to Bed. Clocks put back one hour.

Thursday 23ʳᵈ. Cabin very comfortable and extremely nice Steward. Did washing, all of us feeling well. Lovely day with cool breeze. Hairdo at 5 pm. Captains cocktail party before dinner. An elderly man who died during the night of Wed/Thurs was buried at sea at 8-30pm. Clocks put back 30 minutes.

Friday 24ᵗʰ Beautiful warm with gentle breeze. Sat on deck and did knitting and reading. Ditto after lunch. Then a cup of tea followed by boat drill. Bought some more carved animals and changed South African notes for Sterling. Clocks go back 30 minutes again then we are G.M.T. No Priest on board this journey. There are not so many young people on board as there were on our way out. 200 Farmer's Weekly and Femina tour Party on board and 114 from previous voyage. Cough very troublesome. Played bingo.

Saturday 25th. Very lazy day, reading and knitting. Vaal Derby with Ascot Hat Parade.
Sunday 26th. Lazy day again. Overcast and hot. Sunny later in the day. Community singing after dinner.
Monday 27th. Crossing the line ceremony. Very hot. Children's fancy dress parade. Tombola. Saw school of porpoises.
Tuesday 28th Ship stopped at 5-30 to take on injured seaman from Cape Town Castle. Not so hot today but sunny and warm with breeze. Visit to Bridge after lunch. Use of all the instruments explained. Fancy dress parade followed by dancing. Exhibition dance. Bought Spirits to take home.
Wednesday March 1st. "Windsor Castle" passed. Lazy all day.
Thursday Lazy day. Called at Las Palmas. Goods brought on board.
Friday Left 2-30am. Stayed up to see ship leave harbour. Went to cinema.
Saturday Packing, reading and hairdo. Much colder and very windy. Distribution of prizes at dance.
Sunday quiet day and quiz in evening.
Monday Arrived Southampton 7am.'

They told us it was the holiday of a lifetime and it had been a real joy to them to see Peter in the places where he had worked for so long.

Michael and David both continued as partners in the business. One of the regular customers was Lady Romula Russell, who used to come in wearing enormous hats and buy cigars as gifts for her family. She said her family used to tease her about the hats and she always took it well, she was always a very pleasant customer.

One lunchtime, Michael was alone in the shop. A man wanted to buy cigars and asked if he would take a cheque. Michael said 'Yes.' and now says he should have suspected because when the man gave his address he spelt the county Somerset with two M's! Later it was found that that man had 'done the town' going into almost all the shops in the town and swindling them all. This was before the days of cheque guarantee cards.

In September 1968 the retail price maintenance on Tobacco Products was ended. This led to many shops cutting prices on cigarettes etc. so David persuaded Harrison to begin to expand the lines that were sold in Harrison & Simmonds.

It was about this time that Michael decided he would like to be a teacher so when he heard that Polhill College was taking mature students he applied and after doing a years study at evening school he was accepted.

113

Michael left the shop in August 1969 and did three years training to be a teacher. He worked at first at Goldington Road Junior School and after a couple of years transferred to St Gregory's RC School at Biddenham. Michael worked there until he had a heart attack in 1984 when he retired from teaching.

We now had three children and money was tight, so I applied to go back to work as a staff nurse, part time, to eke out our income, as we were living on a grant while Michael was training. I worked on the Special Care Baby Unit at North Wing Hospital, three evenings a week and Saturday afternoons and I really enjoyed being back in the hospital environment.

It was a shock to us all when we learnt early in 1970 that Nathaniel Harrison was ill, and even more of a shock when Madeleine died in August, and Harrison so soon afterwards in December 1970. After Madeleine died Harrison had moved in with Aunts Ede and Nell at 87 Goldington Road.

It was from there that Michael took him into the hospital on 9th December. Harrison had deferred his pension until he was seventy. This was his seventieth birthday so on the way they stopped at the Post Office and he drew his pension for the first and only time. He died a few days later with Peter at his side. From the local paper:-

'Round Table founder Dies aged 70
One of the founder members of the Round Table in Bedford, Mr Nathaniel Harrison Simmonds, died on Wednesday aged 70. Mr Simmonds of 87 Goldington Road, Bedford, died in the North Wing of Bedford General Hospital. He leaves four sons and a daughter. He moved to Bedford in 1928 and in partnership with his uncle started the tobacconists' business of Harrison and Simmonds, which will now be carried on by his son David. Until his death Mr. Simmonds was on the board of governors of St. Joseph's School. He was also a member of two church organisations - The Knights of St. Colomba and the St. Vincent de Paul Society. His eldest son Peter, who works at a missionary school in South Africa, was with his father when he died.'

In Harrison's will he left sums of money to Peter and John to help their religious orders. He also left smaller sums to Liliane, Ernie Shiner and to me. He left £50 to each grandchild, which was given as National Savings Certificates.

The residue of the estate was left to be distributed equally between Mary Shiner and Michael and David Simmonds. Much of this money remained invested in Harrison and Simmonds so Harrison was still caring for the business even after his death.

Harrison's legacy to Michael and me, enabled us to move to a larger house in July 1971 six weeks before our twins were due. Dominic Hugh and Maria Aideen Simmonds were born on August 13th 1971. We were able to buy a four bedroomed house without a mortgage thanks to Harrison.

Nathaniel Harrison Simmonds and Madeleine were both buried in Elstow Abbey churchyard near to their relations.

Their tombstone reads:-

'IN LOVING MEMORY OF OUR DEAR PARENTS MADELEINE AND NATHANIEL SIMMONDS WHO DIED 23RD AUG. AGED 64 & 16 DEC. AGED 70. 1970.'

Corrections p.114:
"Michael left the shop in August 1968.....
he had a heart attack in 1985"

In 1969, David knowing that his Dad was ill, had asked his brother-in-law John Maund if he would like to come and work with him. John thought about it and eventually decided to join David. John was married to David's wife's sister Mary Joe nee Pace. They had three children Sarah, Jonathan and Anna. John started at the shop while Harrison was still working in early 1970.

The new shop at 80 High Street, Bedford

John remembers that at 78a High Street they had a trap door under the chair where Harrison used to write. It opened upwards and revealed steps down to a low cellar that stretched right under the shop. Michael remembered seeing ancient invoices with stamps of George V. There was also a tiny little room upstairs that had rumour of a ghost. 78a later became absorbed into 78 High Street that Michael remembers as Peter Dominic's wine shop after the Stones Radio Co left.

In 1971 the lease was running out so David and John decided to move the shop up to 80 High Street where it is today. John Maund told me about the move, which took place over a spring bank holiday weekend. They had access to the new shop for a week or so before so had been able to fit the cupboards etc as they wanted but they could not move the stock until after the shop shut on the Saturday evening.

Everybody in the family was roped in to help. The first thing to be moved was the old counter. It was loosened from its moorings and lifted onto a sort of platform with four pram wheels. Then it was manoeuvred out of the door with some difficulty, as it was very heavy. It was placed in the same position in the new shop. Then all the left hand side of the shop with all the fixtures and fittings the tobacco jars etc were moved into the same position as in the old shop, but the shop was now twice as wide.

They spent all day Sunday (apart from going to church) and all day Monday arranging the stock and the shop opened on Tuesday morning in the new premises and many customers did not realise the shop had moved! They even asked what had happened to the old gas lighter! (in the old shop permanently alight on the counter!)

The new shop apart from being twice as wide was also longer and had a back entrance into Lime Street, with outbuildings where some of the staff kept their bikes while at work. It had a small office behind and a tiny cloakroom/kitchen. There is also car parking space allocated to the premises.

The rent which had been fixed for all those years suddenly jumped from £40 four times a year (a total of £160 per year at 78a) and increased tenfold to £1700 per year at 80 High Street. That deal that Harrison had made with old Mrs Covington had been a real bargain.

The Bedfordshire Times had a feature with the headline 'Suddenly they've moved -- as if by magic.' The feature showed pictures of the original shop in 1928 and a photo of the new shop with Will Maund(John's father), John Maund, Peggy Canny, Edith Mousley and David Simmonds. 'With a touch of sorcery a familiar High Street landmark vanished last weekend, only to reappear at double its size a few paces further up the road. But like all the best magic, the removal of this tobacco store --- established 100 years ago--- was the result of careful planning and the ability to invoke a special atmosphere. Totally repudiating the chrome and veneer of a plastic age, owner David Simmonds and partner John Maund have gone all out to preserve the nostalgic Dickensian flavour of their old premises by retaining a large number of the wooden fittings and decorations. The oak window and door fittings of the new shop blends happily with

117

the well worn dark shelves that have held Bedfordian's tobacco and cigars for the past hundred years.' The paper goes on for several more paragraphs about the expansion of the business and the family concerned. The writing is surrounded by adverts of the various pipes, lighters etc sold in the shop.

The newspaper picture of the staff outside the new Harrison and Simmonds. From the left: Will Maund, John Maund, Peggy Canny, Edith Mousley & David Simmonds.

John & David went to trade fairs and discussed what lines they could branch out into. John made the rack for the walking sticks and one year while David was away in Greece visiting Liliane's relations, John built a walk in Cigar Humidor and the Humidor cost £18 70p. In June 1973 they bought a filing cabinet for £20 and Taylor's of old Bond Street sent a Rep in one day and they ordered some pots of shaving cream that retailed at £8-00.

From an old analysis book that has survived from 1973, opening balance (in Metric since 15 Feb 1971) for April £70 50p cash with £367 14p in bank. The daily takings varied between £150 and £300 per day. Coffee was

86p and the window cleaner now gets 50p! A trip to London to a trade fair cost £3 and the wages were £31. Firms mentioned include Papworth Industries, Puddefoot, Bowes, Comoy, Marshall & Co, Vantage Leather Goods, Creative Metals, & International Tobacco Sales. Eastern Electric gets £67 36p and Players and Ronson are still the two largest payouts.

In October 1973 they paid F. G. Harrison £6-00 for 'Goods.' This was George Harrison, Nathaniel Harrison Simmonds' cousin, who had run a tobacconist shop in Luton that was also formerly owned by the Covington family. George had bought his shop from Harry W. Covington with his legacy from the sale of the chemists shop in Salisbury that was begun by his grandfather Joseph Painter Harrison, who was also grandfather to Nathaniel Harrison Simmonds.

My aunt Marian Taylor remembers going into George Harrison's shop to buy cigars for her brothers. She had no idea at that time that I, her niece, would marry into that family! George's shop closed about this time with the building of the new Arndale Shopping Centre in Luton.

Strangely my uncle Ted Taylor was also involved with the Arndale Centre. Ted had retired from Vauxhalls and then there was a fire in the offices of the architects who were building the Arndale centre. Ted Taylor answered the advertisement and got the job of sorting out all the half burnt drawings and redoing them so that the job could continue.

The glass bowl engraved by Michael March

In 1974 the list of employees in Bedford included Mrs Edith Mousley (Aunt Ede still doing the books each week) £7-00 weekly, Mrs M. Canny (Peggy) £18-00 weekly, Mr. Will Maund (John's father) £10-00 weekly and Mr. Michael March (Liliane's cousin) £95-15 monthly all before tax!

In November Mr. J Simmonds is included at £5-00 weekly, this is probably David's son James, an actor who has often helped out when he was 'resting.'

Michael March who started at the shop in 1974, remembered being asked to engrave a large glass bowl. He had to measure it carefully and work out the exact distances between each letter and then tackle the job, engraving by hand knowing that one mistake would ruin the whole bowl! He did it on the pen counter and the lady was very pleased with the results. Michael March did a lot of the engraving on pens and other articles which have been a good source of income over the years.

Michael March did not like to waste anything, so one day he brought a bone to the shop. When a man came in with two large dogs Michael said 'Do your dogs like bones?' Immediately the two dogs started barking madly so Michael rushed to get the bone and gave it to them.

Partners David Simmonds, John Maund and Michael March

Michael March said they were always laughing in the shop. Each customer was pleasant and they appreciated the 'quaint old fashioned atmosphere.'

It was about this time that Hockliffe's was taken over by W H Smith & Co and moved from the High Street, Bedford, into the new Harpur shopping centre. This meant that there was no outlet in the High Street for the leather goods that they had sold, so Harrison & Simmonds started to stock purses and wallets. They took over a postal tobacco business from their friend and business colleague R. Walbourn Smith who was retiring.

They started to stock Mont Blanc pens when they were first imported in the mid nineteen seventies. They sold Du Pont Lighters at about the same time. They also sold Lilliput Lane models, ornaments of all types, Chess sets, walking sticks, pocket watches and all sorts of other models. Later they began to stock Ronsons razors, electric shoe polishers, and cordless telephones.

At a trade fair in London David saw a political chess set featuring the political leaders of the day, including Harold Wilson, Margaret Thatcher, Ted Heath and Enoch Powell. David bought it and the following spring the chess set was on display in the window during the election campaign. It was featured in the Beds Times as one or two of the MP's shown were not standing, it made people stop and look in the window and gave them a laugh.

Inside 80 High St, from left: John Maund, Peggy Canny, Michael March, Will Maund and David Simmonds.

In June 1978 there was a feature in the Bedfordshire Times headed 'Smokers of the world ignite. 'The feature shows a photo of all the staff, John,

Peggy, Michael March, Will Maund and David, and talks of how Harrison & Simmonds are still selling tobacco. *'The shop in Bedford High Street doesn't only exude the pungent smell of tobacco far removed from the type that is machine stuffed into economy brands, it bears that mark of discrimination and quality which has been largely stubbed out by the twentieth century'*

The article tells of all the other lines now being sold by Harrison & Simmonds and also shows a picture of John weighing out some tobacco and smoking his pipe. The feature is surrounded by adverts for pipes and pens, tankards and chess sets and other lines sold by the shop, with congratulatory messages.

David continued his Dad's giving to support charities: Rotary Club 2-00 and London Association for the Blind £2-00 and, he also paid out £14-40 to 'Home Counties News' for advertisements perhaps. New firms mentioned include Waddington's, Louis Glass, Scala Products, Friborg & Treyer, Palmer Sharkey, & Morris & Morris. They paid £21-75 for 'Goblets,' and to Thornton Baker, the Accountants, £146-50.

David Simmonds and Peggy Canny serving

Harrison & Simmonds were founder members of the Association of Independent Tobacconists. David was Chairperson of the Association for a while. Harrison & Simmonds were featured in their in-house magazine 'Tobacco' in January 1980.

The feature told how David when faced with cut - price rivals nearby had decided to branch out into postal sales of Havana cigars. So in 1978 he had begun advertising in various Sunday papers. At first David was concerned in case he was taking trade from other specialist tobacconists. So the orders were very carefully mapped with different coloured pins showing first and later orders. Thus they saw that the orders were coming from mainly country districts where it was difficult to get to a specialist in cigars. The article included pictures of David and Peggy in the shop.

122

During this time John Simmonds (Brother Simon, Order of Friars Minor, still working in Yorkshire) was employed on a part time basis doing pipe repairs for the shop and his wages helped the Franciscan Order. Some of the entries in the analysis book in 1976 include 'John Simmonds, Heads for pipes £12-00' and earnings £120 per month. One of his letters has survived from that time. It is dated   7/9/80

'My dear John M.

Thankyou for cheque and petty cash and also for Hardcastle address. Re invoices for August, I apologise for not telling you that I was holding back those entered for Comoy, as I had the last one to complete work on. I enclose them all now therefore you can settle me up for them on next months account. This should be the last from Comoy no.s 3507-3512.

Many thanks from John   From the Workshop Osmotherly.'

Bro.Peter SDB, David, Mary, Michael and John
(Bro. Simon OFM) Easter 1980

The investors in the business at this time included M. Shiner, Ellen Simmonds, Margaret Canny, M. J. Maund, L. M. Simmonds & E. Mousley.

In that same year Peter was over on holiday and the four brothers and their sister were together in David & Liliane's garden at Easter when the last photo was taken of them all together.

Mrs Margaret (Peggy) Canny finally finished working in the shop in November 1984 after over thirty years of faithful service. Peggy Canny died the following year.

Katy Robbins (John Maund's niece) began to work in the shop about this time. The money was kept in a drawer at the back of the shop.

They had used a cash register in the old shop but did away with it in the new shop. One day David pulled out the drawer too far and the money ran all over the floor! David said to Katy 'when did you last do that?' Katy was indignant. Katy later worked in the Cambridge shop.

After over thirty years as a Franciscan brother, John Simmonds was ordained as a Priest on 15th. March 1986 at Canterbury. Father Simon OFM now works in Stratford in the East End of London. He was Spiritual Adviser to the Secular Franciscan Order for many years so Michael & I have seen quite a lot of him, in his official capacity. He is always full of fun capping puns and cracking jokes even when giving spiritual talks! He is greatly loved by all who know him.

Bro. Peter came over from South Africa to attend John's Ordination and so by God's mercy, he was here when Mary died and was able to be at her funeral. He was also here in England for Ernie Shiner's Funeral in August 2000.

14   The Cambridge Shop

In the early eighties business was variable so it was decided to expand and they looked around for another shop. They heard of premises being rebuilt in Cambridge and decided to open a second shop there. In 1985 a new branch of Harrison & Simmonds was opened in St Johns Street, Cambridge and this did very well.

The Cambridge Harrison and Simmonds in St John's Street

The shop was in a prime position right across the zebra crossing from St.John's the Round Church. They employed a manager Richard Zdziaski, and various members of the family and staff commuted everyday, and they also employed some Cambridge people.

Most of the fittings and fixtures in the new shop were designed by John Maund, and made and fitted by Nicholas Shiner, Mary's eldest son, now with his own carpentry business. Some of the cupboards came from Richard Burr's shop in Midland Road Bedford and spent time in David's garage until the time came to take them to Cambridge. The cupboards and showcases were done throughout in rich red mahogany and the shop had a spiral staircase in the centre leading to the basement show room. David had an old ambulance that was used by all the family for transporting stuff to and fro. We borrowed the ambulance for a family camping holiday that summer.

Inside the Cambridge Shop showing the spiral stair case to the basement

They had a tiny camera fitted so they could keep an eye on what went on downstairs. It is a beautiful shop. John and David each spent half the week in Bedford and half in Cambridge. John's daughter Sarah Maund, his son Jonathan and his nieces Katie & Louise Robbins also worked in Cambridge and later David's daughter Christiane, and his son James also worked at the Cambridge shop. Our son Dominic began to work in the shops in 1988 when he was seventeen, David's son Matthew began in 1990.

The business bought two cars to transport the family staff to and from Cambridge. Dominic used to go over often and so did Matthew. A typical week shows Mon. David & Pat, Tues. John & Rich'd, Wed. Rich'd & Pat, David later, Thurs. Rich. Pat. & John, Fri. Jonathan & Rich'd, Sat. David Jonathan and James.

The staff used to leave little notes for each other in the shop diary and sometimes add tiny drawings and other hieroglyphics! In Jan 1990 there is note saying that David and Matthew will be away on 10, 11, & 12th. Under the dates are Yahoo! Yipee! and Whoo!

On 21st April a note to Matthew 'Dear Mafu, You are to be a good hard worker & look after Richard & the shop for me until I get back, otherwise there will be all sorts of trouble in July when I return to sort things out! Love Tamsin' Above this in different hand is written 'No more Tamsin Oh Dear!' This is typical Simmonds banter.

A Tobacco pouch from the time when Harrison & Simmonds had the second shop in Cambridge

John Maund remembered one day when a large Japanese family came into the shop. Grandpa, parents & grown up children. They all asked to look at different things and after a lot of deliberation they decided on a selection of goods and then said they would return later. John thought it was all in vain. However late in the day one of the family returned and paid for the whole order in cash and took the whole lot away to a taxi waiting outside. That one family spent £1,200 in one go!

On 15th October 1990 a note says 'Its Richard's and Tamsin's birthdays! Get your wallets out!' In December another note 'Maffoo's back!' with a tiny sketch of Matthew beside it. One week the staff went as follows:- Mon. Jonathan Tamsin Matthew, Tues. Matthew Tamsin James, Wed. Rich James Tamsin, Thurs Rich James John, Fri Rich James Tamsin, Sat Rich John, Matt, Tamsin & Sarah.

John remembers selling a seat stick to Peter Ustinov, and Prince Edward came in once with some other young people but he did not buy anything. Jeffrey Archer came in two or three times and bought pens and once he left his American express card behind!

In August 1990 the Cambridge shop paid out as follows Comb/pen cases £8-00, Milk 56p, Battery 73p, Wax Polish £1-59, light bulb 2-95, Post and stamps £67-45, Timber £36-48, Petrol £15-00, nails & screws £3-60, Groceries £1-37, Elastic bands 1 lbs. £4-96, Chess Booklets £2-86, washing up liquid 58p and the window cleaner got £8-00!

There was a trader in Bedford called 'Toys 86.' Knowing that Harrison & Simmonds had a shop in Cambridge, he suggested that he could supply Harrison and Simmonds with 'Burago' 1/18 scale model cars to sell in the Cambridge shop. These cars were sold in Cambridge and later also in Bedford after Toys 86 closed.

The Cambridge business was doing very well, but it was a bind having to find and pay for parking for the cars every day and there were problems with the staff.

As David put it 'With the internet business expanding and the Cambridge expenses increasing it became less and less of a joy, so when the offer came I was glad to take it.'

So the Cambridge shop was sold in 2000 when David was offered a very good deal. The stock in Cambridge was sold and went for more then they expected. John had a heart attack after reading that letter! He retired soon after.

So Harrison & Simmonds now only have the one shop in the High Street in Bedford.

Michael Simmonds had suffered a heart attack in September 1985 and decided to retire from teaching so David invited him back as a simple shop assistant in the Bedford shop. This was good as he did not have the worries of responsibility, but could enjoy the camaraderie of the shop and he is a good salesman. Michael is always careful to keep up with the cleaning and dusting, restocking shelves and changing towels etc. He brings towels and tea towels home for me to wash.

In 1986 Harrison & Simmonds was nominated for a 'Service with a Smile Award.' They were nominated by Mrs Margaret Wilson of Putnoe and there was a feature in the Beds. Times & Citizen.

Mrs Wilson wanted to thank them for *'Their many years of polite cheerful and friendly service every week no matter the weather.'*

Bernard McGinty, Mrs Wilson, Michael March and Michael Simmonds

It was Bernard McGinty a friend who worked in the shop for some years who suggested McGinty's Mixture. Sometimes there were packets of unsold tobaccos that were discontinued so Bernard suggested saving up all these oddments and blending them into a cheap tobacco and it was called after him.

In the early 1980's the Bedford shop was expanded further, taking over the ground floor part of the solicitors offices that had been upstairs as well as behind the shop. At this time the old counter with the fixtures and fittings behind, were moved to the back of the shop, but the old Tobacco jars etc are still there and they still sell Harrison's blends of tobacco. There are two stock rooms and an office plus a kitchen and cloakroom at the back of the shop.

Dominic Simmonds serving at the back of the extended shop.

Harrison & Simmonds have quite often been featured in the papers. From the 'Express' 8 August 8 1986 a picture of David in the shop with the headline '*Snuff this out now!*

Bedford tobacconist David Simmonds is campaigning for a crackdown on sales of cigarettes to children under 16 years of age. Mr. Simmonds who has a shop in the High Street, is one of thousands of shopkeepers around Britain now backing a tobacco industry initiated scheme to axe illegal cigarette sales to children. The campaign supported by the government, features a series of distinctive stickers for In-shop display which make it clear that the retailer will not sell cigarettes to children.

Mr. Simmonds said "Any children seeing these stickers will realise that the retailer is not prepared to sell them cigarettes. This helps the staff in shops who often don't have time to argue with children, many of whose ages are difficult to judge. It also shows the public that the tobacco industry is not just interested in selling cigarettes to anyone ------ despite what is sometimes claimed by the extremist anti-smoking groups..'

There was a feature in the Beds Times in June 1988 after sixty years of Harrison & Simmonds. It showed a picture of John Maund, David Simmonds, Michael March and William Maund, John's father who also helped in the shop for some years. Harrison is shown on the right in a picture taken in 1959, and a picture of the old shop. The headline was

'Business is booming 60 years on.

Sixty years ago cigarette smoking was regarded as highly fashionable. How times have changed! Today smoking is very much "tres mal" and smokers are continually urged to kick the habit. So it is not surprising that many small tobacconists have been forced to close their doors as sales plummeted. But diversity has proved a lifeline to Harrison and Simmonds, one of Bedford's most highly respected and established family businesses. And this year the firm celebrates its diamond anniversary having weathered the storm by developing the business into an upmarket gift shop mainly for men.

It was in 1928 that Ernest Harrison a jeweller from Tunbridge Wells, and his young nephew moved to Bedford and bought a tobacconists shop in the High Street. That same week the Bedfordshire Times published a supplement celebrating the birth of John Bunyan 300 years previously; Tarzan and the Apes was showing at in the Picturedrome; and the new memorial Hall in Stewartby was opened.'

The account continues for another couple of columns with the history of the shop as I am telling it only very brief!

On Monday 14 October 1990 Dominic arrived on his bicycle to open the Bedford shop and went round the back to put his bicycle in the shed in the back yard and saw a body hanging there. A young man had committed suicide! At first Dominic thought it was a stunt of some kind and then another man, who worked at the Trustee Savings Bank, came and told Dominic that he had phoned the police. Dominic was only nineteen and had never seen a dead person before, so after being interviewed by the police he was sent home to recover from the shock. John remembered that he was not allowed to park round the back until the police had finished.

Later on, driving over to Cambridge one day, Dominic witnessed a bad accident and he said although he saw blood and brains all over the road it did not affect him as much as the suicide had. Dominic used to take the day's mail round to the main Post Office in Dane Street every evening and that is how he met his wife Sarah Russell, as she was also in the queue with mail from her work place. Both Dominic and Matthew were made partners with David after John retired.

In the early nineties the large Pipe sign that hung outside the High Street shop was stolen during rag week. So Michael made a new sign and there was a feature when the new sign went up, in October 1992.

'They're fuming! Holy smoke! Put that in your pipe and smoke it! That's the message from the proprietors of Harrison and Simmonds tobacconist's who are finally replacing the sign stolen from the shop by thieves. To save themselves being the butt of everyone's jokes they have coughed up for a new sign. Partner David Simmonds, a well known thespian of these parts, said "The sign had been in the pipeline for ages and we were delighted when it finally arrived.'

John Maund and David Simmonds with the new pipe sign made by Michael Simmonds

Michael March left the shop in 1993 and went to work at the Bedford Museum. He was a partner with David and John from 1980 to 1993.

There are also notes about family events in the shop diaries- 15 September 1990, Jane Simmonds Wedding should Michael or David go? (Jane is Christopher Simmonds daughter.) Eventually it worked out that it was I, Anne Simmonds who took Aunt Edith Mousley to that wedding! Dominic's first son Cameron was born on 1 February 1993 this is noted next to 'Police Statement D.C.Wright' about one of the burglaries?

On 23 May 'Sarah & Alex wedding, John Off' He had to be off to give his daughter away! In May 1993 'Betty Harrison Funeral' Betty was George Harrison's widow, who had been living in a nursing home at Silsoe for some years.

Dominic Simmonds with his son Cameron and father Michael Simmonds who was cleaning a lighter with methylated spirit, hence the bottle!

There is a note of an investment from 'Hannings' in September 1993. 'Hannings' was a business run by our son-in law. If any of the family have a sum of money to invest we always think of Harrison & Simmonds.

There have been several burglaries at Harrison and Simmonds over the years. Once the burglars made their entry through the ceiling from the upstairs during the time it was empty. When the alarm went off one of the burglars broke his leg in his rush! Michael March remembered two chaps in their late thirties, coming in and looking around. They took a couple of Du Pont lighters.

One morning a man came in and wanted to buy a quantity of cigarettes. He asked to pay by card. The name on the card was J. Warwyn. Now Michael had taught a boy at school with that name, and this man looked very different, so Michael rang the bank to check and they told him the card had been stopped!

One day Michael missed his penknife and thought he must have lost it. However a few weeks later a man came in to have a penknife repaired and Michael recognised it as the one he had lost. He told the man he thought it was his and the man told him that he had bought it from someone in Church Square. Michael told him to keep it as Michael had a new one anyway. Later there was phone call from Social services saying that this man wanted to return the things he had taken, Michael told them that he had told the man to keep it. They said he would also like to return the ballpoint pen. Michael had not even missed the pen!

Brian Morris with David Simmonds and John Maund at the back of the shop where the original counter and fixtures are now.

One of the characters who has been a friend and helper to the family and in the shop for many years is Brian Morris. He helps in so many ways and is always willing to run errands or help with carpentry or with serving or any other job he can do.

Brian built a wooden platform/ramp outside our back door at home, so that people could get to the toilet outside without having to step down and then up again. This was invaluable after my mother had a stroke and was in a wheel chair and also later when I had my knees replaced.

One day Michael was stocking shelves at the front of the shop when a man came in. Michael said 'Do you want serving?' The man said 'Yes' So Michael told him if he went to the back of the shop there would be someone to serve him. The man went to the back and complained that Michael had refused to serve him!

Another time Michael Simmonds came back from his lunch just as Dominic was serving a man who was taking a long time to make up his mind between two pocket watches. Dominic turned to put one away and the man grabbed the other one and ran out of the shop and down the High Street. Michael ran after him shouting "Stop Thief!"

The man turned into the Arcade with Michael in close pursuit. Another man saw what was happening and as Michael was tiring, he took up the pursuit, calling "Stop Thief." Another man at the far end of the Arcade put out his arms across the exit. The thief threw the watch into a bin and escaped.

Meanwhile the staff at Clayton's Menswear shop in the Arcade had alerted other shops over a security radio link and the thief was later arrested while shop lifting in another shop. The watch was retrieved from the bin and returned to Harrison & Simmonds.

After 'Toys 86' closed down in the 1990's Harrison & Simmonds began to sell the model cars in Bedford. This model department has since expanded with Dominic's interest in cars especially racing cars. The diary notes Thunderbird, Corvette convertible, Mini Cooper S, V.W.Beetle, Ford T. Van, assorted colours. Chevrolet Bel Air, Mercedes Benz 300 SL, Porsche 356a coupe, Rolls Royce Phantom, Ferrari set 12 varied colours. The above were all in one order in 1992

It was also Dominic who suggested selling 'Disc World', 'Enchantica' Myth & Magic and Egyptian figures. Another order from 1992 includes from 'Pendragon' Tyrannosaurus Rex, Apatosaurus, Stegosaurus, Styrocosaurus, and Triceratops etc. The shop also sells models of aeroplanes, tanks, farm machinery etc.

The Internet now plays a big part in the business with an 'On line Virtual tour of the shop' and customers ordering from all over the country. The packing up and posting of the day's orders is a big job, for all the staff every afternoon. Matthew Simmonds is responsible for the website and the updating of the lists etc. Most of the engraving is now done by Matthew Simmonds with the computer so it is less risky as it is almost all done by machine not by hand as in Michael March's time.

When Michael Mortimer was about to retire and closed his shop 'Mortimer's' in the Arcade he was very grateful to David Simmonds. Harrison and Simmonds not only took 2/3rds of his stock, but also paid for it within days, which helped Michael Mortimer to retire peacefully with no worries.

In September 2003 Bro. Peter Simmonds celebrated the 50th. Anniversary, of his profession as a Salesian Lay Brother. Peter had taught woodwork and metal work in a school when he first arrived in Cape Town. This was the time of Apartheid so it was a school for white boys only. However once the regime changed later on, they were allowed to teach children of all races. Peter was Head master for some time but he much preferred actually being with the boys and not having so much paper work.

Peter spent many years running the Repository which supplies candles linens and other altar furnishings to churches throughout South Africa. Peter designed a candlestick that can be adjusted to hold candles of different sizes. This became known in Cape Town as "The Jaws candle stick". He has now patented a new version of this and it sells well. He also worked at a nearby parish of Lansdowne for some years.

After Apartheid was done away with it was Peter who suggested 'The Learn to Live' project. The Salesian Institute takes in homeless boys off the street and teaches them life skills and trades so that they can be responsible citizens. They often have about twenty boys mostly teenagers living in the Institute. They are taught carpentry, metal work, leatherwork, and printing.

After eighteen months or so the boys are helped to find a job and when they leave they are supplied with a wooden ten-foot square house with a corrugated iron roof and a built in bed, table, and wardrobe. This they have erected near their work or family and thus they have a secure home of their own and can become responsible citizens.

Michael and I were privileged to be able to visit Cape Town to represent the family in the celebrations. There was a special Mass with the Archbishop of Cape Town and over forty priests, followed by a big party. Lots of tribute were paid to Peter for his devoted service to all the children he had served over the years.

Peter in reply told us that he never expected to get to that point. As his parents had both died by age seventy he did not expect to live any longer. He added with a smile that he had recently been given a different room. It was the one that Father X and Brother Y had lived in, and they have both since died, so he said 'I think of it as the departure lounge!' This raised a good laugh from Peter's confreres. Peter will be eighty in November 2007, he is currently writing a booklet on the history of the Salesians in South Africa.

In the summer of 2006, on the recommendation of the accountants, Harrison and Simmonds became a Limited Company. This is for financial reasons. David is now the Chairman and managing director. Dominic and Matthew are now directors.

Harrison & Simmonds Staff in 2006. Michael, David & Matthew Simmonds, Thomas Shiner, Dominic Simmonds and John Barnes

The staff who have worked for Harrison and Simmonds number approximately 40 over the past eighty years and thirty of these people are relations or connected by marriage. Most of the others have already been friends of the family before they come to work in the shop.

There have been five generations of the family involved over the past eighty years. The first Generation was Ernest Harrison.

The second generation were Nathaniel Harrison Simmonds and Edith Mousley & also Madeleine Simmonds who helped out part time in the forties and fifties. Will Maund also really belongs to this generation

The third generation are Peter (who worked for but not in the shop), John, Michael, David and Liliane Simmonds, John Maund, Michael March, also Marie Joe Maund & Lena Pace, two of Liliane's sisters.

The fourth generation include our son Dominic and David's son, Matthew, Christiane (David's daughter) who worked in the Cambridge shop for some years before she was married and her husband John Barnes now on the permanent staff. David's older son, James, our Clare, Francis, Maria, & Catherine Simmonds, (who all worked in the shop, while still at school as Saturday and holiday helpers) also John Maund's daughters Sarah & Anna Maund, his son Jonathan Maund and his nieces Katie & Louise. I also include Nicholas Shiner who fitted the Cambridge shop.

The fifth generation is Mary's grandson Thomas Shiner who worked in the shop for several summers while still at school and more recently joined the permanent staff.

The staff now in 2007 include David, Matthew & Dominic Simmonds who are directors, John Barnes (David's son-in-law) Simon White (a friend of Dominic's) and Thomas Shiner (Mary's grandson.) as well as Michael Simmonds still working part time, to cover days off etc.

Will the shop continue into the sixth generation? David has four grandsons and Michael & I have ten grandchildren from four of our children, and another expected in October 2007 so there is hope that one or other of the next generation may carry on the family business.

It is strange to think that if Nathaniel Simmonds had not died in 1906 then his son Nathaniel Harrison might have spent his life selling books in Salisbury and Harrison and Simmonds might never have existed. The shop is still very much part of the family after eighty years of service to the people of Bedford.

And now you know why it is called Harrison and Simmonds.

140

Biscay Bay of 109
Bishop of Rochester 52.
Bishop of Salisbury 30
Blair Atholl, Scotland, 57
Bland Rev. T. H. 27
Blenheim Palace 14
Bognor Regis 49
Bologna 93
Bollington 99.
Boots The Chemist 56
Bournemouth Dorset 26, 51
Bourne Rev. G.H. 38
Bowyer The Misses K and F. 70
Bowes 119
Bristol Siddeley News 48
British American Tobacco Co. 83.
Broadmead School Luton, 4
Bromham 3, 9, 90.   Bridge 97.
Primrose Cottage, Grange Lane 9- 11

Brown Anne Catherine nee Napier 25-6
Brown Bros 31
Brown Buster & Kit 89, 93, 97.
Brown Edward 25
Brown Edwin Lewis 26
Brown Eliza later Simmonds
  23-6, 32, 35-6.
Brown Mattie Elizabeth later
  Simmonds 26
Brown Thomas 23.
Brown's 31
Bryan C/Obs. 82
Bryant & May 83
Buckingham. 13, 53
Market Square 13
White Hart Inn 13
Buckingham Bailiff of 13
Buckingham Duke of 14

Buckton Arthur , Landlord of Wheatsheaf
  Inn 16, 17.
Bunyan John 131
Burdett Fraser Dorothy Nancy later
  Harrison 52
Burden Albert Thomas (Bert) 17, 30,
53-4, 98.
Burden Alice nee Harrison 16-7, 19-20,
30-1, 53- 55, 98.
Burden Albert Ernest 53, 63, 70.
Burdon Phyllis Emily 17, 53-4, 70.

Burt Henry & Co 76.
Burago 128
Burr Richard 126
Bustin Phyllis nee Hayward later King
  63-6, 69, 74, 79, 87, 101.
Bustin Reg. 69, 101.
Butcher Ada Emily nee Waddington
  59- 60.
Butcher Ethel 59-61.
Butcher George 59-60.
Butcher Violet Emily (Madeleine) later
  Simmonds 2-3, 5-6, 9-11, 59-62, 66-7,
  69-70, 74 , 79-80, 81, 84-5, 88-90, 93-4,
  98-101, 109-13, 114-5, 138.
Buzz Bomb 78
Cadena Cafe 97, 102.
Cambridge St Johns Street 125-7.
St John's Church 125

Canny Mrs. Peggy (Margaret) 3- 6, 83,
  85, 107, 117-123.
Canterbury 124.
Canvin's Bedford 2
Cape Town Archbishop of 136
Cape Town South Africa, 6, 10,
  93, 109,111, 136
Captain Cuttle 2, 90-1.
Carlton Shoe Co, High St Bedford 63
Carroll 87.
Carter Patterson 82, 86.
Cartilidge Mrs. 70.
Chalk Farm, 174 Regents Park Road, 44.
Chambers 31
Chapman Obs. 82
Charter Pipes 108
Charles I, 13.
Charles Comins & Co. Chrted Accts 44.
Charles Fairmorn (UK) Ltd 101.
Chartres 93.
Chevrolet Bel Air 135
Chilworth 95.
'Chords Major & Minor' 22
Churchman 79, 87.
Christopher 83.
Civic Gas Co. The 79
Civil Defence Duties 74
Clacton 67
Clapham 78
Clarke. Mr. 77.

144

Morris Mrs. (Cape Town) 111
Morris & Morris 122
Mortimer's 79, 87, 136.
Mortimer Kevin 90
Mortimer Michael 9, 79 87-8, 136.
Mortimer Pat 79, 87, 108.
Mossey Rev Father 77
Mousley Edith nee Simmonds (Aunt Ede)
    3, 9, 29-33, 37, 40, 42-6, 51, 61, 92-3,
    104-6, 118, 123, 138.
Mousley Frank 44-6
Mousley Maurice 46
Mousley Patricia (Pat) 3, 45, 92, 98-9
    102, 104-5,
Mummery Mr. A.A. 70
Munton C/Obs. 82
Myth & Magic 135
Napier Anna Catherina nee
    Tregonwell 25
Napier Anne Catherine later Brown 25-6
Napier Rev.Edward 25
Napier Martha nee Gorringe Troake 25
Napier Thomas Tregonwell 25
National Employers Mutual, War Risk 83
National Employers Mutual
    Insurance 83, 86
Neate Mr. Edwin J. 70
Neate Mr. Lewis W. 70
Neate Obs/O. 82
Newport Pagnell Bucks 46, 98.
Newton Tony Wilts 23
New Zealand 51
Nicholson George 56
Nightingale Obs/O. 82
Norris Isabella later Simmonds 23
Norwich 59
O'Brian Father 100.
Observer Corps 73-4, 82.
Observer Close 73
Ogden 79, 87.
Oliver Twist 91
O'Neil Nora 89-90.
Ord W.W. MD. 38
Orleans 93
Orlik House of 83, 107-8.
Oppenheimer 79, 87.
Osmotherly, Yorkshire 95, 123.
Otley Yorkshire. 60.

Owen's School 75
Oxford 28, 90.
Pace Lena 138.
Pace Liliane later Simmonds 5-6, 9,
    107, 123, 138.
Pace Marie Joe later Maund 116,
    123, 138
Page Rose later Sanger 26
Painter John 14
Painter Pleasant later Harrison 14, 15.
Palmer Sharkey 122.
Papworth Industries 119
Paris 93
Parkers 87.
Parker Pen Co. 85
Peacock Mr. Auctioneer 63
Peggotty 91
Pendragon 135
Pepys Samuel 15
Percival Obs/O. 82
Perks Obs. 82
Peter Dominic's Wine shop 116.
Peter Stokkeybye Tobacco's 102.
Pickwick 2, 91.
Players 63, 76, 81, 79, 119.
Plewman Obs. 82
Polhill College 113.
Pope Pius XII 93
Porsche 356a coupe 135.
Portland Pipe Co 83
Portsmouth 51-2.
Power pak 99.
Powell Enoch 121.
Prince Edward 128.
Proposal 24
Puddefoot 119
Princess Mary's Village Homes
    39, 41-2, 50.
Pusey St.Francis School 53-4.
Porton Wilts. 35
Pryer Mr. and Mrs. A. V. 70
Queens Club 44
Queen Elizabeth 69
R101 Airship 65
R.A.F. Comfort Fund 82
Radcliffe Infirmary in Oxford 48.
Railway Company 82
Raleigh Bike 78.